JUMBLE®

MADNESS

T0155429

crazy for jumbles®

Henri Arnold, Bob Lee, and Mike Argirion

TRIUMPH
B O O K S
CHICAGO

This book is available at special discounts
for your group or organization.

For further information, contact:

Triumph Books
601 South LaSalle Street
Suite 500
Chicago, Illinois 60605
(312) 939-3330
FAX (312) 663-3557

ISBN 1-892049-24-4

Printed in the USA

CONTENTS

---

classic

Jumble® Madness #1 - #25

Page 1

---

daily

Jumble® Madness #26 - #160

Page 27

---

challenger

Jumble® Madness #161 - #180

Page 163

---

answers

Page 184

JUMBLE®

MADNESS

classic
puzzles

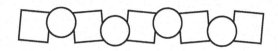

JUMBLE®

Unscramble these four Jumbles, one letter to each square, to form four ordinary words.

FRUOM

DEACK

REPERF

CROONB

Print answer here

THIS BLOW WAS GOT FROM A SCUFFLE.

Now arrange the circled letters to form the surprise answer, as suggested by the above cartoon.

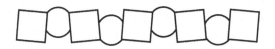

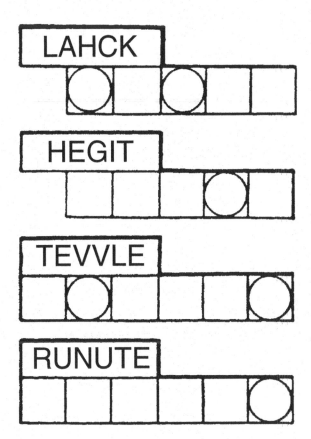

JUMBLE®

Unscramble these four Jumbles, one letter to each square, to form four ordinary words.

LAHCK

HEGIT

TEVVLE

RUNUTE

Print answer here

None better exist

ONE—THAT MIGHT BE WORTH MORE THAN ANY OF THE OTHERS.

Now arrange the circled letters to form the surprise answer, as suggested by the above cartoon.

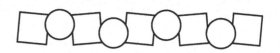

JUMBLE®

Unscramble these four Jumbles, one letter to each square, to form four ordinary words.

FRIGE

YONIS

SAMOUF

JICTEN

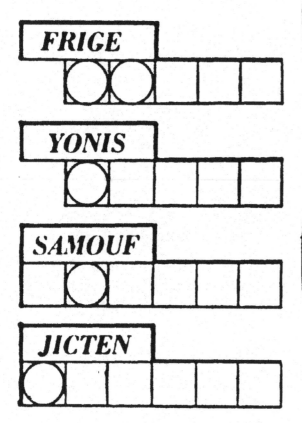

How barbaric!

HOW ODD THAT IT MIGHT BE SQUARE!

Now arrange the circled letters to form the surprise answer, as suggested by the above cartoon.

Print answer here

JUMBLE®

Unscramble these four Jumbles, one letter to each square, to form four ordinary words.

HEWEL

TREEB

ALOONG

STOUBE

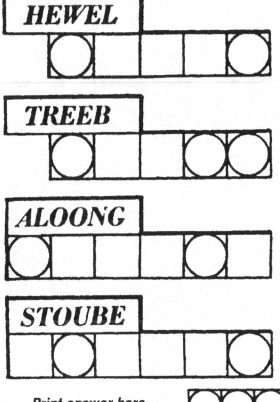

WHERE SOME PEOPLE MANAGE TO KEEP THEIR WEIGHT DOWN.

Now arrange the circled letters to form the surprise answer, as suggested by the above cartoon.

Print answer here   THE

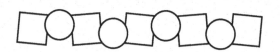

JUMBLE

Unscramble these four Jumbles, one letter to each square, to form four ordinary words.

RECEL

GOGSY

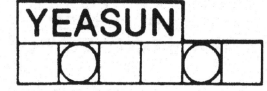

YEASUN

DUGIED

EVEN BETTER THAN A CLOSE FRIEND.

Now arrange the circled letters to form the surprise answer, as suggested by the above cartoon.

Print answer here A  ONE

PUZZLE
6

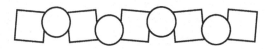

JUMBLE.

Unscramble these four Jumbles, one letter to each
square, to form four ordinary words.

KECHE

YIKTT

KERROB

CLINAG

But I LIKE it!

WHAT THE NAVY
RECRUIT GOT OUT
OF BOOT CAMP.

Now arrange the circled letters to form the surprise
answer, as suggested by the above cartoon.

Print answer here   A ⬡⬡⬡ ⬡⬡⬡⬡

7

JUMBLE

Unscramble these four Jumbles, one letter to each square, to form four ordinary words.

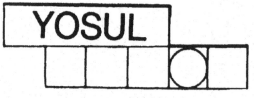

YOSUL

DIGUL

CANOBE

LAMORF

They married too young

WHAT PUPPY LOVE IS SOMETIMES THE BEGINNING OF.

Now arrange the circled letters to form the surprise answer, as suggested by the above cartoon.

Print answer here A

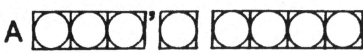

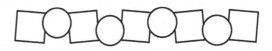
JUMBLE®

Unscramble these four Jumbles, one letter to each
square, to form four ordinary words.

TANBO

DANGL

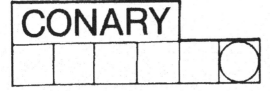

CONARY

VAHLED

WAH!

WHAT NO
UPRIGHT PERSON
WOULD DO.

Now arrange the circled letters to form the surprise
answer, as suggested by the above cartoon.

Print answer here

Unscramble these four Jumbles, one letter to each square, to form four ordinary words.

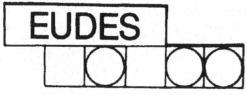

EUDES

SUGES

YAPNOC

DALLIP

Whew! That was close!

DID HANGMEN CARRY OUT SUCH SENTENCES?

Now arrange the circled letters to form the surprise answer, as suggested by the above cartoon.

Print answer here  ONES

Unscramble these four Jumbles, one letter to each
square, to form four ordinary words.

Famous philosopher

PORRI

VUEMA

GROFTE

TUCLED

WORDS YOU MIGHT
GET FROM
VOLTAIRE.

Now arrange the circled letters to form the surprise
answer, as suggested by the above cartoon.

Print answer here " ◯ ◯◯◯◯ ◯◯◯ "

JUMBLE®

Unscramble these four Jumbles, one letter to each square, to form four ordinary words.

TUDOO

OUSIP

NOOPUC

MUSSIE

WHAT A LADLE IS.

Now arrange the circled letters to form the surprise answer, as suggested by the above cartoon.

Print answer here A

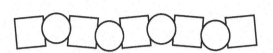

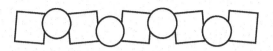

JUMBLE®

Unscramble these four Jumbles, one letter to each
square, to form four ordinary words.

OPEEL

TOROB

SUSTLY

FUNCED

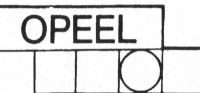

He just doesn't have
a green thumb

WHAT LIFE WAS
FOR THAT UNLUCKY
GARDENER.

Now arrange the circled letters to form the surprise
answer, as suggested by the above cartoon.

Print answer here NO ⬡⬡⬡ ⬡⬡ ⬡⬡⬡⬡⬡

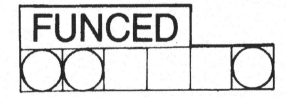

JUMBLE®

Unscramble these four Jumbles, one letter to each square, to form four ordinary words.

GEALE

VERAB

SMIDOH

UNGATH

WHAT YOU MIGHT GET FROM A DEBATER.

Now arrange the circled letters to form the surprise answer, as suggested by the above cartoon.

Print answer here   " ◯◯◯◯◯◯◯ "

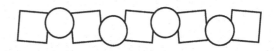

JUMBLE®

Unscramble these four Jumbles, one letter to each square, to form four ordinary words.

NILER

SUMIN

GARCHE

NAPMEN

METAL DEVICES
THAT HELP KEEP
LOCKS IN PLACE.

Now arrange the circled letters to form the surprise answer, as suggested by the above cartoon.

Print answer here

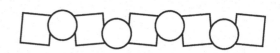

JUMBLE®

Unscramble these four Jumbles, one letter to each square, to form four ordinary words.

CEPEA

LYMAN

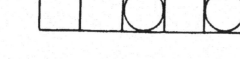

DILIOB

BYSMOL

Maybe he should see a shrink

HE COULDN'T REMEMBER — WHAT THIS WORD MEANT.

Now arrange the circled letters to form the surprise answer, as suggested by the above cartoon.

Print answer here

" "

Unscramble these four Jumbles, one letter to each
square, to form four ordinary words.

NOYOL

YICTH

STYJUL

LADRIA

HOW THEY BENT
THEIR KNEES.

Now arrange the circled letters to form the surprise
answer, as suggested by the above cartoon.

Print answer here   " ◯◯◯◯◯ – ◯◯ "

JUMBLE

Unscramble these four Jumbles, one letter to each square, to form four ordinary words.

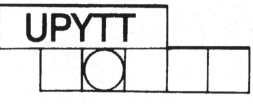

UPYTT

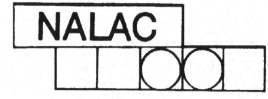

NALAC

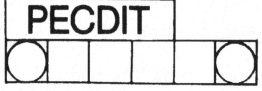

PECDIT

ARXOTH

WHAT THE MANICURIST'S CUSTOMER WAS GETTING.

Now arrange the circled letters to form the surprise answer, as suggested by the above cartoon.

Print answer here

 OF

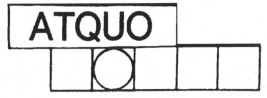

Unscramble these four Jumbles, one letter to each square, to form four ordinary words.

ATQUO

ELCHE

BLAMME

It's amazing!

WHAT COLOR COULD THE BLOUSE POSSIBLY BE?

OSOYUJ

Now arrange the circled letters to form the surprise answer, as suggested by the above cartoon.

Print answer here

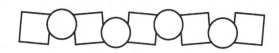

JUMBLE.

Unscramble these four Jumbles, one letter to each square, to form four ordinary words.

TOUHY

FRUOM

SITMIF

CACTEN

Work when you please

A JOB FOR SOMEONE WHO'S WELL-PADDED.

Now arrange the circled letters to form the surprise answer, as suggested by the above cartoon.

Print answer here

" "

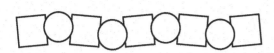

JUMBLE

Unscramble these four Jumbles, one letter to each
square, to form four ordinary words.

YOSIN

TEJEC

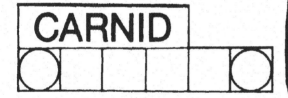

CARNID

DOURNA

Trouble is we
spoiled him

WHAT THE LOAFER
WHO WAS BORN WITH
A SILVER SPOON IN
HIS MOUTH HASN'T
DONE SINCE.

Now arrange the circled letters to form the surprise
answer, as suggested by the above cartoon.

Print answer here

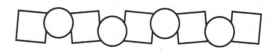

Unscramble these four Jumbles, one letter to each square, to form four ordinary words.

SUMEA

ILETT

NILJEG

GAYMIB

WHAT A GIRL SOMETIMES WEARS AT THE BEACH.

Now arrange the circled letters to form the surprise answer, as suggested by the above cartoon.

Print answer here A

Unscramble these four Jumbles, one letter to each square, to form four ordinary words.

NERAV

VALIT

MEEGRE

A FRUITFUL SOURCE OF INFORMATION.

SCIBEP

Now arrange the circled letters to form the surprise answer, as suggested by the above cartoon.

Print answer here **THE**

 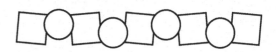

JUMBLE®

Unscramble these four Jumbles, one letter to each square, to form four ordinary words.

NORPE

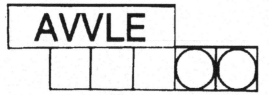
AVVLE

TRUFOH

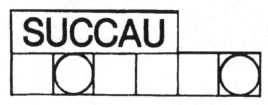
SUCCAU

HOW THEY CLAPPED
THEIR HANDS WHEN
SHE SANG.

Now arrange the circled letters to form the surprise
answer, as suggested by the above cartoon.

Print answer here  THEIR

Unscramble these four Jumbles, one letter to each
square, to form four ordinary words.

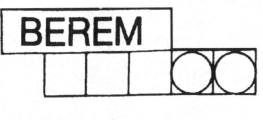

BEREM

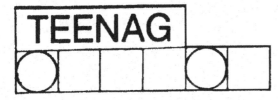

LIDAP

TEENAG

WHAT HE HAD TO DO
EVERY TIME SHE HAD
AN ACCIDENT IN
THE KITCHEN.

GLEANT

Now arrange the circled letters to form the surprise
answer, as suggested by the above cartoon.

*Print answer
here*

 IT FOR

25

JUMBLE®

Unscramble these four Jumbles, one letter to each square, to form four ordinary words.

SYSEM

THYFE

GITHEY

PENMAD

Agreed?   Agreed!

YOU MIGHT SEE EYE TO EYE WITH SOMEONE WHO'S THIS.

Now arrange the circled letters to form the surprise answer, as suggested by the above cartoon.

Print answer here **THE** ⬡⬡⬡⬡⬡ ⬡⬡⬡⬡⬡⬡

JUMBLE®
MADNESS

daily
puzzles

JUMBLE.

Unscramble these four Jumbles, one letter to each square, to form four ordinary words.

GUCOH

MUJOB

BELUCK

WHOANY

Ugh!

WHAT THAT INVISIBLE MAN DEFINITELY WAS NOT.

Now arrange the circled letters to form the surprise answer, as suggested by the above cartoon.

Print answer here ◯◯◯◯ TO ◯◯◯◯ AT

JUMBLE®

Unscramble these four Jumbles, one letter to each square, to form four ordinary words.

CREMY

REDON

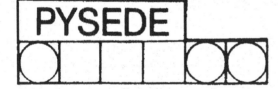

PYSEDE

CASIMO

THAT GOSSIPY DRESS-
MAKER APPEARED
TO KNOW ONLY
THIS ABOUT LIFE.

Now arrange the circled letters to form the surprise answer, as suggested by the above cartoon.

Print answer here THE "  "

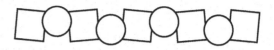

JUMBLE®

Unscramble these four Jumbles, one letter to each square, to form four ordinary words.

NAYGO

FEMAL

EXDULE

THE WITCH ENDED UP HERE AFTER SHE DID THIS.

RAWHEL

Now arrange the circled letters to form the surprise answer, as suggested by the above cartoon.

Print answer here ⬡⬡⬡⬡ OFF THE ⬡⬡⬡⬡⬡⬡

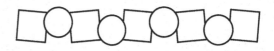

JUMBLE®

Unscramble these four Jumbles, one letter to each square, to form four ordinary words.

VICLI

NORIB

HALMYN

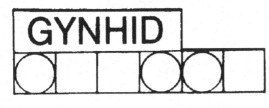
GYNHID

HE HAD TO
WORK LIKE
A HORSE BECAUSE
HIS BOSS WAS
ALWAYS DOING THIS.

Now arrange the circled letters to form the surprise answer, as suggested by the above cartoon.

Print answer here "  "

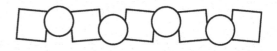

JUMBLE®

Unscramble these four Jumbles, one letter to each square, to form four ordinary words.

CYKAT

RUGPO

FASTIE

ENOMAY

DISCO

He owns the ___
place, too

WHAT YOU MIGHT
SEE A BOUNCER
THROW.

Now arrange the circled letters to form the surprise
answer, as suggested by the above cartoon.

Print answer here A

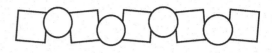

JUMBLE®

Unscramble these four Jumbles, one letter to each square, to form four ordinary words.

YENED

DAPAT

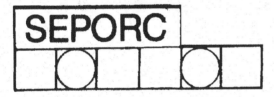

SEPORC

TURSIM

THAT EXPENSIVE COUNTRY CLUB HAS THIS.

Now arrange the circled letters to form the surprise answer, as suggested by the above cartoon.

Print answer here MORE  THAN

JUMBLE

Unscramble these four Jumbles, one letter to each
square, to form four ordinary words.

YUINT

NOLFE

KLUSCE

SLIFSO

WHAT SOME SKIERS JUMP TO.

Now arrange the circled letters to form the surprise
answer, as suggested by the above cartoon.

Print answer here "◯◯◯◯◯◯◯◯◯◯◯"

JUMBLE®

Unscramble these four Jumbles, one letter to each
square, to form four ordinary words.

BAYSS

YAFFT

DINBAT

NIGDIH

HOW A BOXER
MAKES MONEY.

Now arrange the circled letters to form the surprise
answer, as suggested by the above cartoon.

Print answer here

OVER

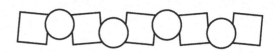

JUMBLE®

Unscramble these four Jumbles, one letter to each square, to form four ordinary words.

ZARUE

FECAH

DARFIA

QUAPEL

WHAT SOME SO-CALLED "DINNER PARTIES" SORT OF ARE.

Now arrange the circled letters to form the surprise answer, as suggested by the above cartoon.

Print answer here " ◯◯◯ – ◯◯◯◯◯◯ "

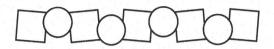

JUMBLE®

Unscramble these four Jumbles, one letter to each square, to form four ordinary words.

STOIF

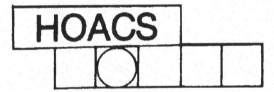
HOACS

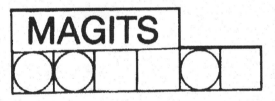
MAGITS

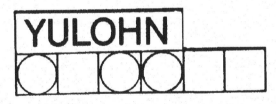
YULOHN

Come and get me!

WHAT THE GUY WHO BRUSHED HIS TEETH WITH GUNPOWDER DID.

Now arrange the circled letters to form the surprise answer, as suggested by the above cartoon.

Print answer here ⬚⬚⬚⬚ HIS ⬚⬚⬚⬚⬚ OFF

JUMBLE®

Unscramble these four Jumbles, one letter to each
square, to form four ordinary words.

VIRTE

RETEB

BORREB

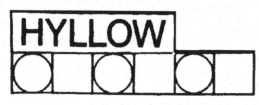

HYLLOW

It's supposed to
be a wall

HOW A
MASON LEARNS
HIS TRADE.

Now arrange the circled letters to form the surprise
answer, as suggested by the above cartoon.

Answer BY " ☐☐☐☐☐☐ " & ☐☐☐☐☐☐

Unscramble these four Jumbles, one letter to each square, to form four ordinary words.

ROODE

POLEE

LETTAC

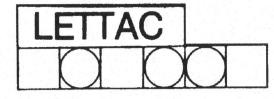

CYNAGE

SHE LIKES MEN WITH SOMETHING TENDER ABOUT THEM, ESPECIALLY WHEN IT'S THIS.

Now arrange the circled letters to form the surprise answer, as suggested by the above cartoon.

Print answer here

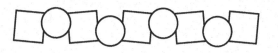

JUMBLE.

Unscramble these four Jumbles, one letter to each square, to form four ordinary words.

RODUG

VORLE

ABBOMO

DURECE

We women have been pushed around for too long

WHAT KIND OF A HUSBAND DID SHE FINALLY MARRY?

Now arrange the circled letters to form the surprise answer, as suggested by the above cartoon.

Print answer here ONE  TO "  "

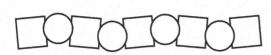
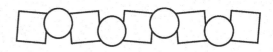

JUMBLE.

Unscramble these four Jumbles, one letter to each square, to form four ordinary words.

RASEE

DICHE

RAHNGE

DIBITT

Will be glad when they can get to the country

WHAT THERE WAS IN THAT CROWDED CITY.

Now arrange the circled letters to form the surprise answer, as suggested by the above cartoon.

Print answer here A

OF

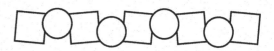

JUMBLE®

Unscramble these four Jumbles, one letter to each square, to form four ordinary words.

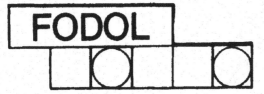

FODOL

COTTE

REGEME

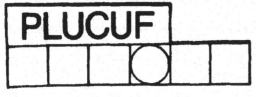

PLUCUF

Gen-u-wine 24 karat

WHAT YOU MIGHT GET WHEN THE WOOL IS PULLED OVER YOUR EYES.

Now arrange the circled letters to form the surprise answer, as suggested by the above cartoon.

Print answer here

" "

Go ahead—he won't bite you

PRIVATE

AN ENTERPRISING
PERSON SHOULD
NOT BE BACKWARD
IN GOING THERE.

JUMBLE®

Unscramble these four Jumbles, one letter to each square, to form four ordinary words.

PUTER

DUBON

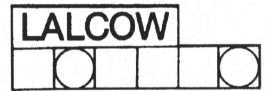

LALCOW

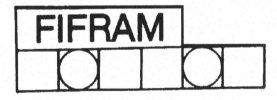

FIFRAM

Now arrange the circled letters to form the surprise answer, as suggested by the above cartoon.

Print answer here

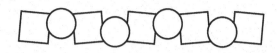

JUMBLE.

Unscramble these four Jumbles, one letter to each square, to form four ordinary words.

FIDOR
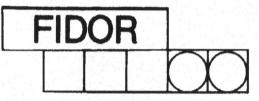

TABEA

WELBIA
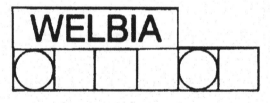

JUINER
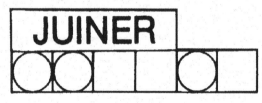

WHAT THEY CALLED THAT NUTTY ORNITHOLOGIST.

Now arrange the circled letters to form the surprise answer, as suggested by the above cartoon.

Print answer here

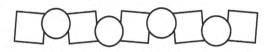

JUMBLE.

Unscramble these four Jumbles, one letter to each square, to form four ordinary words.

YAKLE

RIFAY

GLABEN

TROGOT

So glad
that cold
spell is over

WHAT SPRING SHOULD
BRING AFTER
A ROUGH WINTER.

Now arrange the circled letters to form the surprise answer, as suggested by the above cartoon.

Print answer here

" ☐☐ - ☐☐☐☐ "

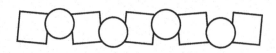

JUMBLE®

Unscramble these four Jumbles, one letter to each
square, to form four ordinary words.

LUFTO

DENIK

UNCANE

BRUBRE

Yeah, I got all de angles

But just
look at
that guy!

EITHER A
BOXER CARRIES
OUT HIS PLANS TO
BEAT HIS OPPONENT,
OR HE'S THIS.

Now arrange the circled letters to form the surprise
answer, as suggested by the above cartoon.

Print answer here

JUMBLE®

Unscramble these four Jumbles, one letter to each
square, to form four ordinary words.

BALEF

KICCH

QUAPOE

NATIVY

Print answer here

He may be overdoing it

APPARENTLY, A GUY
WHO EATS AND DRINKS
TOO MUCH WOULD
RATHER BE A GOOD
LIVER THAN THIS.

Now arrange the circled letters to form the surprise
answer, as suggested by the above cartoon.

 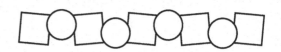

Unscramble these four Jumbles, one letter to each square, to form four ordinary words.

ORRAM

SOPIE

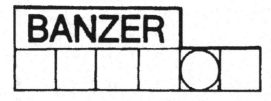

BANZER

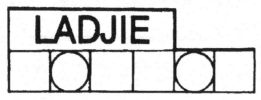

LADJIE

THIS HELPS MANY A GOLFER TO IMPROVE HIS SCORE.

Now arrange the circled letters to form the surprise answer, as suggested by the above cartoon.

Print answer here AN

JUMBLE

Unscramble these four Jumbles, one letter to each
square, to form four ordinary words.

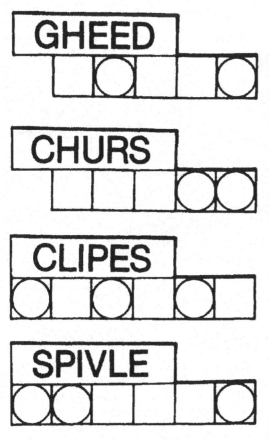

GHEED

CHURS

CLIPES

SPIVLE

Doesn't have a brain
in his head

WHAT HE WOULD
BE IF HE SAID
WHAT HE THOUGHT.

Now arrange the circled letters to form the surprise
answer, as suggested by the above cartoon.

Print answer here

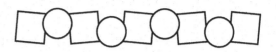

JUMBLE

Unscramble these four Jumbles, one letter to each square, to form four ordinary words.

You'll sleep like you never did before

WHAT THE SALESMAN SAID THAT BARGAIN BED WAS.

TAFAL

YAGUD

CLYMAL

BELUBB

Now arrange the circled letters to form the surprise answer, as suggested by the above cartoon.

Print answer here A " ⬡⬡⬡⬡⬡ - ⬡⬡⬡ "

JUMBLE.

Unscramble these four Jumbles, one letter to each square, to form four ordinary words.

TALGO

TESCA

ZEABAL

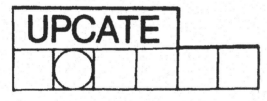

UPCATE

Let's cool it

THE MEMBERS OF THE JURY ARE SUPPOSED TO "SIT" UNTIL THEY DO THIS.

Now arrange the circled letters to form the surprise answer, as suggested by the above cartoon.

Print answer here

" ◯◯◯◯◯◯ "

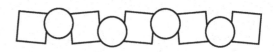

JUMBLE

Unscramble these four Jumbles, one letter to each square, to form four ordinary words.

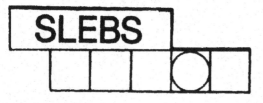

SLEBS

CUNOE

HOW A NEST
EGG MUST
BE FEATHERED.

WARDTY

THROOC

Now arrange the circled letters to form the surprise answer, as suggested by the above cartoon.

Print answer here WITH ⭕⭕⭕⭕ " ⭕⭕⭕⭕ "

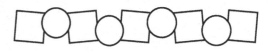

JUMBLE®

Unscramble these four Jumbles, one letter to each square, to form four ordinary words.

NORIG

CHOUP

WHAIGE

SELUNS

THE ONLY THING THAT KEPT HIM FROM MAKING A FAST BUCK AT THE RACE TRACK.

Now arrange the circled letters to form the surprise answer, as suggested by the above cartoon.

Print answer here A

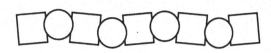

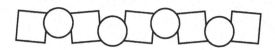

JUMBLE®

Unscramble these four Jumbles, one letter to each square, to form four ordinary words.

ICCOL

SOITH

MAPCEN

BLOORE

WHAT PIERCES YOUR EAR WITHOUT LEAVING A HOLE?

Now arrange the circled letters to form the surprise answer, as suggested by the above cartoon.

Print answer here

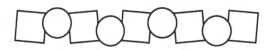

JUMBLE®

Unscramble these four Jumbles, one letter to each square, to form four ordinary words.

GINCI

BYMAL

TIGBLE

CEEPIA

HE TOLD THEM HE WAS JUST WHAT THE DOCTOR ORDERED.

Now arrange the circled letters to form the surprise answer, as suggested by the above cartoon.

Print answer here

A

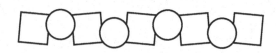

JUMBLE®

Unscramble these four Jumbles, one letter to each
square, to form four ordinary words.

DONEM

CAPIN

FLATUR

LUFUES

WHAT THE
TOW TRUCK WAS
TRYING TO DO
AT THE AUTO RACE.

Now arrange the circled letters to form the surprise
answer, as suggested by the above cartoon.

Print answer here ◯◯◯◯ A ◯◯◯◯◯ ◯◯◯◯

JUMBLE.

Unscramble these four Jumbles, one letter to each square, to form four ordinary words.

RUFOR

TOHRT

ZERBAL

GOINID

WHAT AN EXCITING "MATCH" WILL DO FOR THE FANS.

Now arrange the circled letters to form the surprise answer, as suggested by the above cartoon.

Print answer here ◯◯◯◯◯ A ◯◯◯◯

JUMBLE®

Unscramble these four Jumbles, one letter to each square, to form four ordinary words.

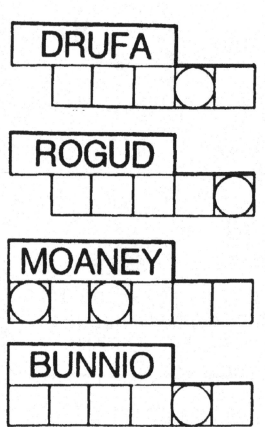

DRUFA

ROGUD

MOANEY

BUNNIO

THE RULES FOR MAKING MONEY WON'T WORK UNLESS---

Now arrange the circled letters to form the surprise answer, as suggested by the above cartoon.

Print answer here

JUMBLE®

Unscramble these four Jumbles, one letter to each square, to form four ordinary words.

IMMAX

DYSUK

WAMIDY

KLEETT

Not for me

THE EMBEZZLER'S FAVORITE MORNING DRINK.

Now arrange the circled letters to form the surprise answer, as suggested by the above cartoon.

Print answer here " ⟳⟳⟳⟳⟳⟳⟳ " ⟳⟳⟳⟳

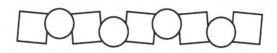

JUMBLE®

Unscramble these four Jumbles, one letter to each square, to form four ordinary words.

KONET

BYLUR

NECTED

SADLIM

I bought this with my prize money

HOME SITES FOR SALE

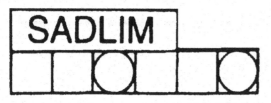

WHAT THE LOTTERY-WINNING REALTOR CONSIDERED HIS PROPERTY PURCHASE.

Now arrange the circled letters to form the surprise answer, as suggested by the above cartoon.

Print answer here "  " OF

JUMBLE®

Unscramble these four Jumbles, one letter to each square, to form four ordinary words.

USTEA

VUCER

FEBRYL

CEVIED

WHEN THEY WATCHED THE STEELWORKERS THE CROWD WAS----

Now arrange the circled letters to form the surprise answer, as suggested by the above cartoon.

Print answer here

61

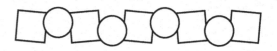

JUMBLE®

Unscramble these four Jumbles, one letter to each square, to form four ordinary words.

KLACH

VOPER

GREFOT

ROHORR

You're on in ten minutes

STAGE DOOR

He never misses a performance

WHAT THE COP MOONLIGHTING AS AN ACTOR WAS KNOWN AS.

Now arrange the circled letters to form the surprise answer, as suggested by the above cartoon.

Print answer here A

JUMBLE®

Unscramble these four Jumbles, one letter to each square, to form four ordinary words.

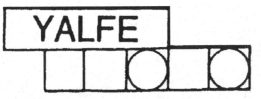

YALFE

CINEE

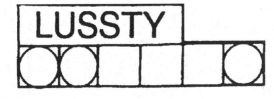

LUSSTY

SMURTE

Thank you, next

WHAT NEW ACTORS BECOME A PART OF.

Now arrange the circled letters to form the surprise answer, as suggested by the above cartoon.

Print answer here THE

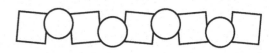

JUMBLE®

Unscramble these four Jumbles, one letter to each square, to form four ordinary words.

TARIE

GREME

ROTRAM

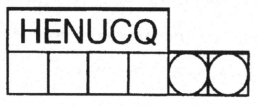

HENUCQ

This is where
he first saw her

She won
him over

WHAT THE
TENNIS PRO
FINALLY DID.

Now arrange the circled letters to form the surprise answer, as suggested by the above cartoon.

Print answer here ⬭⬭⬭ HIS "⬭⬭⬭⬭⬭"

JUMBLE®

Unscramble these four Jumbles, one letter to each
square, to form four ordinary words.

GAANP

GALLE

DRENER

WEDOMA

He does it all by himself

WHAT THE
COWBOYS CALLED
THEIR COOK.

Now arrange the circled letters to form the surprise
answer, as suggested by the above cartoon.

*Print answer
here*   **THE** ⬡⬡⬡⬡ ⬡⬡⬡⬡⬡ - ⬡

JUMBLE

Unscramble these four Jumbles, one letter to each
square, to form four ordinary words.

SHIWK

YAWNT

DAILNG

DIBORM

All fixed

WHERE MONEY
GOES WHEN THE
PLUMBER COMES.

Now arrange the circled letters to form the surprise
answer, as suggested by the above cartoon.

Print answer here ◯◯◯◯ **THE** ◯◯◯◯◯

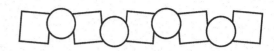

JUMBLE®

Unscramble these four Jumbles, one letter to each square, to form four ordinary words.

LELIS

ZIRPE

CHORBO

NATILE

Remember -- a penny saved is a penny earned

TEACHING KIDS TO SAVE IS THIS.

Now arrange the circled letters to form the surprise answer, as suggested by the above cartoon.

Print answer here   "〇〇〇〇〇〇〇〇〇〇"

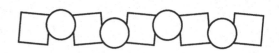
JUMBLE.

Unscramble these four Jumbles, one letter to each square, to form four ordinary words.

YACKT

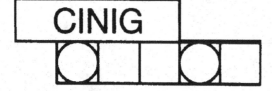
CINIG

WORDSY

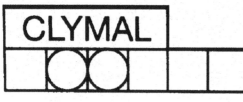
CLYMAL

It's as big as a room

BROWSERS WELCOME

OFTEN SEEN AT A MODEL HOME.

Now arrange the circled letters to form the surprise answer, as suggested by the above cartoon.

Print answer here

JUMBLE®

Unscramble these four Jumbles, one letter to each square, to form four ordinary words.

YUINT

PAMCH

NAHDEL

YIKELL

Here... let me help you

WHAT THE CARING BAKER LIKED TO DO.

Now arrange the circled letters to form the surprise answer, as suggested by the above cartoon.

Answer " □□□□ THE " □□□□□□ "

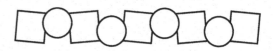

JUMBLE.

Unscramble these four Jumbles, one letter to each square, to form four ordinary words.

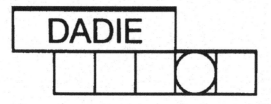

DADIE

SYRTT

CLUDGE

For me?

WHY THE CHILD
PRODIGY ENJOYED
HIS BIRTHDAY.

IMFLYS

Now arrange the circled letters to form the surprise
answer, as suggested by the above cartoon.

Print answer here **HE WAS** " ◯◯◯◯◯◯ "

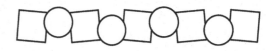

JUMBLE.

Unscramble these four Jumbles, one letter to each square, to form four ordinary words.

No interest for 60 days

Let's give her a bonus

WECIN

DORWS

PERTAT

SPLEET

WHAT THE WORKER GOT FOR SIGNING UP CHARGE CARD CUSTOMERS.

Now arrange the circled letters to form the surprise answer, as suggested by the above cartoon.

Print answer here

 OF

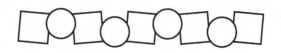

JUMBLE

Unscramble these four Jumbles, one letter to each square, to form four ordinary words.

ELUSO

ORFEC

LAWESE

SPYNAP

Another strike!

He's in the groove

THE REASON HE WON THE BOWLING MATCH.

Now arrange the circled letters to form the surprise answer, as suggested by the above cartoon.

Print answer here HE  A

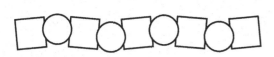

JUMBLE

Unscramble these four Jumbles, one letter to each
square, to form four ordinary words.

VOLCE

KNALB

SLAFTE

POMSIE

WHAT THE DINER
AT THE FISH
RESTAURANT HAD
LOTS OF.

Now arrange the circled letters to form the surprise
answer, as suggested by the above cartoon.

Print answer here ⬡⬡⬡⬡⬡ TO ⬡⬡⬡⬡

JUMBLE®

Unscramble these four Jumbles, one letter to each square, to form four ordinary words.

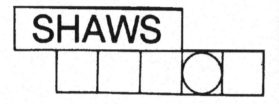
SHAWS

MYMUG

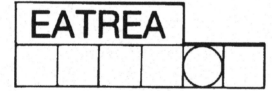
EATREA

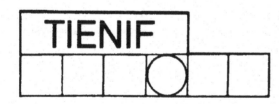
TIENIF

Well, FINALLY we can predict sunshine

WHEN THE FOG CLEARS UP, IT WON'T BE THIS.

Now arrange the circled letters to form the surprise answer, as suggested by the above cartoon.

Print answer here

" ◯◯◯◯ "

JUMBLE

Unscramble these four Jumbles, one letter to each square, to form four ordinary words.

CEENI

RUTYL

VERGAN

DEGEWD

WHAT THE SWIMMING POOL CONTRACTOR DID WHEN BUSINESS FELL OFF.

Now arrange the circled letters to form the surprise answer, as suggested by the above cartoon.

Print answer here

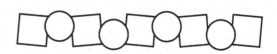

JUMBLE®

Unscramble these four Jumbles, one letter to each
square, to form four ordinary words.

TEENA

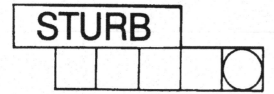

STURB

BEDFAL

STURME

WHO RAIDED
MY VEGETABLE
PATCH?

Now arrange the circled letters to form the surprise
answer, as suggested by the above cartoon.

Print answer here

JUMBLE.

Unscramble these four Jumbles, one letter to each square, to form four ordinary words.

LITTE

YASES

TENCED

ROMMIE

Very eligible — High class

WHAT A SUCCESSFUL BACHELOR DOES, WHICHEVER WAY YOU LOOK AT IT.

Now arrange the circled letters to form the surprise answer, as suggested by the above cartoon.

Print answer here "  "

JUMBLE®

Unscramble these four Jumbles, one letter to each square, to form four ordinary words.

RYHUR

INVEG

DAJEGG

PACALA

AJAX MILK PRODUCTS INC.

WHAT MANY EXPENSES CONNECTED WITH THE DAIRY BUSINESS MIGHT BE.

Now arrange the circled letters to form the surprise answer, as suggested by the above cartoon.

Print answer here

" ⬭⬭ ⬭⬭⬭⬭ "

JUMBLE®

Unscramble these four Jumbles, one letter to each square, to form four ordinary words.

LAGEE

FOIMT

REBAWE

DENGER

WHAT THE CATTLE
RAISER DID WHEN
HE GOT A
BUM STEER.

Now arrange the circled letters to form the surprise answer, as suggested by the above cartoon.

Print answer here  ABOUT

JUMBLE®

Unscramble these four Jumbles, one letter to each square, to form four ordinary words.

ROBIL

EJYTT

YENTIC

BRATIL

Fasten seat belts, we're arriving

STOCKS

MIGHT DESCRIBE THE FEELING YOU SOMETIMES GET WHEN A PLANE DESCENDS.

Now arrange the circled letters to form the surprise answer, as suggested by the above cartoon.

Print answer here

" ◯◯◯ – ◯◯ "

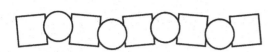

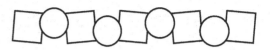

JUMBLE®

Unscramble these four Jumbles, one letter to each square, to form four ordinary words.

BLONE

KADEB

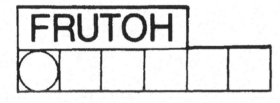

FRUTOH

PIGNUM

WHAT KNOCKING A BALL THROUGH A WINDOW MIGHT BE.

Now arrange the circled letters to form the surprise answer, as suggested by the above cartoon.

Print answer here

"⬡⬡⬡⬡⬡⬡⬡"

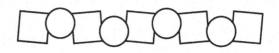

JUMBLE.

Unscramble these four Jumbles, one letter to each square, to form four ordinary words.

KERCE

DOUMI

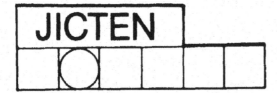
JICTEN

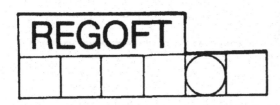
REGOFT

WHAT THE MOUSE SAID WHEN HIS TAIL GOT CAUGHT IN THE TRAP.

Now arrange the circled letters to form the surprise answer, as suggested by the above cartoon.

Print answer here   THAT'S THE ◯◯◯ OF ◯◯ !

 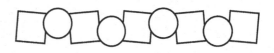
JUMBLE

Unscramble these four Jumbles, one letter to each square, to form four ordinary words.

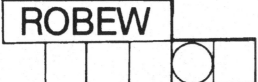
ROBEW

DARTY

FLIXUN

GORCED

WHAT THE TAILOR CALLED HIS PARTNER.

Now arrange the circled letters to form the surprise answer, as suggested by the above cartoon.

Print answer here HIS "  "

JUMBLE®

Unscramble these four Jumbles, one letter to each square, to form four ordinary words.

FINEK

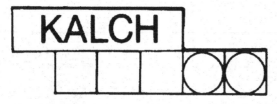

KALCH

TENCCA

SHUBLE

TELLER

Sorry _

WHAT YOU'D EXPECT PEOPLE WITH NO MONEY IN THE BANK TO WRITE.

Now arrange the circled letters to form the surprise answer, as suggested by the above cartoon.

Print answer here

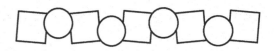

JUMBLE®

Unscramble these four Jumbles, one letter to each square, to form four ordinary words.

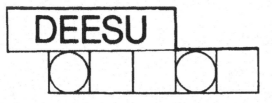

DEESU

YAMEL

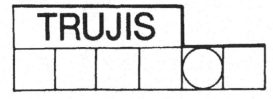

TRUJIS

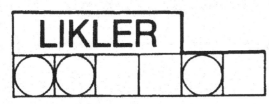

LIKLER

NUMISMATISTS' CONVENTION

WHAT THOSE COIN COLLECTORS ALWAYS GOT TOGETHER FOR.

Now arrange the circled letters to form the surprise answer, as suggested by the above cartoon.

Print answer here OLD ⬡⬡⬡⬡⬡⬡ ' ⬡⬡⬡⬡

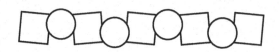

JUMBLE®

Unscramble these four Jumbles, one letter to each
square, to form four ordinary words.

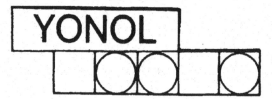

YONOL

RAPPE

RETHOM

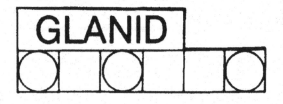

GLANID

Began
with
nothing

Next

A DOCTOR WHO
SPECIALIZES IN THIS
OFTEN STARTS
FROM SCRATCH.

Now arrange the circled letters to form the surprise
answer, as suggested by the above cartoon.

Print answer here

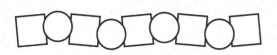

JUMBLE

Unscramble these four Jumbles, one letter to each square, to form four ordinary words.

CRATT

DEHIC

MALBEC

TOEGEA

He's always been a finicky eater

THE FISH REFUSED TO EAT THE WORM ON THE HOOK BECAUSE HE WAS AFRAID THERE MIGHT BE THIS.

Now arrange the circled letters to form the surprise answer, as suggested by the above cartoon.

Print answer here

A ◯◯◯◯◯ ◯◯ IT

JUMBLE®

Unscramble these four Jumbles, one letter to each square, to form four ordinary words.

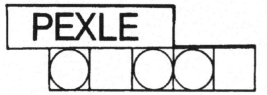

PEXLE

VEREF

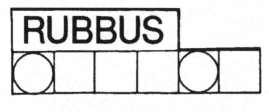

RUBBUS

SHAGAT

THE NEWSPAPERMAN TURNED DRY CLEANER BECAUSE HE DIDN'T BELIEVE IN THIS.

Now arrange the circled letters to form the surprise answer, as suggested by the above cartoon.

Print answer here A ⬡⬡⬡⬡ " ⬡⬡⬡⬡⬡ "

JUMBLE®

Unscramble these four Jumbles, one letter to each square, to form four ordinary words.

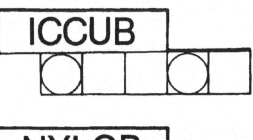

ICCUB

NYLOP

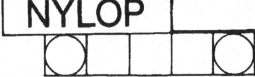

LIGARC

CEVIED

How about it?

CERTAINLY AN OCCASION FOR EATING OUT.

Now arrange the circled letters to form the surprise answer, as suggested by the above cartoon.

Print answer here

A ☐☐☐☐☐☐☐

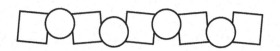

JUMBLE.

Unscramble these four Jumbles, one letter to each
square, to form four ordinary words.

NOROH

FEBOG

ENGOUL

RAUBUE

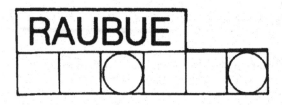

Can't keep up with
'em anymore

THE FELLOW WHO USED
TO RACE CARS QUIT
BECAUSE HE COULD
NO LONGER DO THIS.

Now arrange the circled letters to form the surprise
answer, as suggested by the above cartoon.

Print answer here  FAST

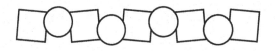

JUMBLE®

Unscramble these four Jumbles, one letter to each square, to form four ordinary words.

SUIGE

TIDEF

YAMBIG

ROCFAT

WHAT HE SAID WHEN HE HEARD HIS NEIGHBOR HAD BOUGHT ONE OF THOSE NEW COMPUTERS.

Now arrange the circled letters to form the surprise answer, as suggested by the above cartoon.

Print answer here

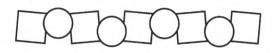

JUMBLE®

Unscramble these four Jumbles, one letter to each
square, to form four ordinary words.

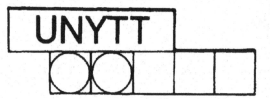

UNYTT

ROALF

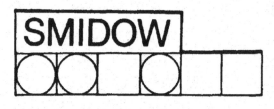

SMIDOW

BEATED

WHAT THAT
FILIBUSTERER
IN THE SENATE
WAS THROWING.

Now arrange the circled letters to form the surprise
answer, as suggested by the above cartoon.

**Print answer
here** HIS " ◯◯◯◯ " ◯◯◯◯◯◯◯

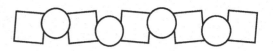

JUMBLE®

Unscramble these four Jumbles, one letter to each square, to form four ordinary words.

TESED

SHOAC

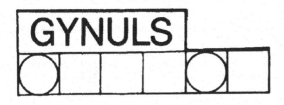

TRUVIE

GYNULS

WHAT DID THE SNAKE WRITE AT THE END OF HIS LETTER?

Now arrange the circled letters to form the surprise answer, as suggested by the above cartoon.

Print answer here

&

Unscramble these four Jumbles, one letter to each square, to form four ordinary words.

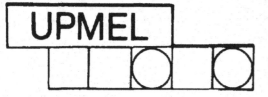

UPMEL

POAKK

MIEPED

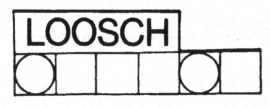

LOOSCH

WHAT THE TIMID SOUL FINALLY DID WHEN HIS BICYCLE WHEEL COLLAPSED.

Now arrange the circled letters to form the surprise answer, as suggested by the above cartoon.

Print answer here

" ⬡⬡⬡⬡⬡ " ⬡⬡

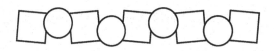

JUMBLE

Unscramble these four Jumbles, one letter to each square, to form four ordinary words.

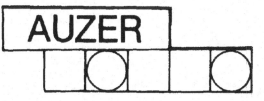
AUZER

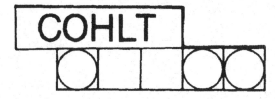
COHLT

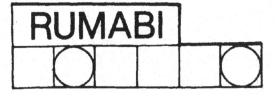
RUMABI

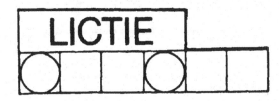
LICTIE

Beautiful move, dearest

WHAT THE MAN FROM PRAGUE CALLED HIS WIFE.

Now arrange the circled letters to form the surprise answer, as suggested by the above cartoon.

Print answer here HIS

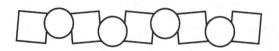

JUMBLE®

Unscramble these four Jumbles, one letter to each square, to form four ordinary words.

KAROC

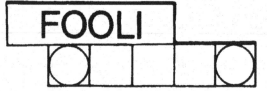

FOOLI

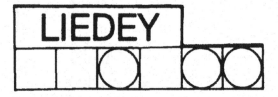

LIEDEY

HINGKT

WHAT A PERSON WHO THINKS BY THE YARD AND DOES BY THE INCH MIGHT GET.

Now arrange the circled letters to form the surprise answer, as suggested by the above cartoon.

Print answer here

 BY THE

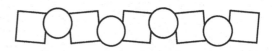

JUMBLE®

Unscramble these four Jumbles, one letter to each
square, to form four ordinary words.

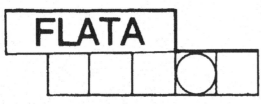
FLATA

TOBAB

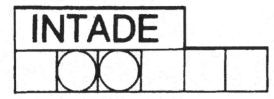
INTADE

ENBATE

"... and in conclusion..."

HOW THAT BUSY
EXECUTIVE FOLLOWED
HIS WORK SCHEDULE.

Now arrange the circled letters to form the surprise
answer, as suggested by the above cartoon.

Print answer here

JUMBLE®

Unscramble these four Jumbles, one letter to each square, to form four ordinary words.

RADAW

ZIPER

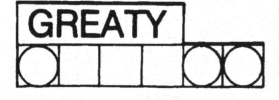

GREATY

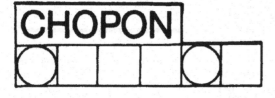

CHOPON

YOU CAN HELP KEEP THOSE FOOD BILLS DOWN WITH THIS.

Now arrange the circled letters to form the surprise answer, as suggested by the above cartoon.

Print answer here

A

JUMBLE®

Unscramble these four Jumbles, one letter to each square, to form four ordinary words.

BILLE

ASSOB

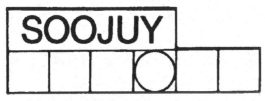

SOOJUY

NAITAT

ALL SHE KNEW
ABOUT COOKING WAS
HOW TO BRING HER
HUSBAND THIS.

Now arrange the circled letters to form the surprise answer, as suggested by the above cartoon.

Print answer here

JUMBLE®

Unscramble these four Jumbles, one letter to each
square, to form four ordinary words.

INYAR

HEWLS

RUJINO

LACKET

NEVER KNOWS WHERE
HIS NEXT CAR
IS COMING FROM.

Now arrange the circled letters to form the surprise
answer, as suggested by the above cartoon.

Print answer here **A**

JUMBLE®

Unscramble these four Jumbles, one letter to each square, to form four ordinary words.

WRONC

TUBIL

FLIDED

VERPOL

WHAT SHE GAVE HIM WHEN HE ASKED WHETHER HE COULD SEE HER HOME.

Now arrange the circled letters to form the surprise answer, as suggested by the above cartoon.

Print answer here A ⬡⬡⬡⬡⬡⬡⬡ ⬡⬡ IT

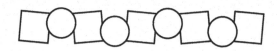

JUMBLE.

Unscramble these four Jumbles, one letter to each
square, to form four ordinary words.

YACKT

NIFYN

SAWLAY

LEWOLF

MR.
JONES

MS.
SMITH

SOME GOSSIPS
WOULD RATHER
LISTEN TO DIRT
THAN DO THIS.

Now arrange the circled letters to form the surprise
answer, as suggested by the above cartoon.

Print answer here

JUMBLE®

Unscramble these four Jumbles, one letter to each square, to form four ordinary words.

WENOM

INJOT

DAGOIA

DOUBIT

Enjoy the mountains

WHAT SOME HUSBANDS WOULD LIKE TO DO WHEN THEIR WIVES GO TO THE COUNTRY.

Now arrange the circled letters to form the surprise answer, as suggested by the above cartoon.

Print answer here " ◯◯ ◯◯ ◯◯◯◯ "

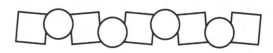

JUMBLE®

Unscramble these four Jumbles, one letter to each square, to form four ordinary words.

AHTEB

NOPUD

NEEVEL

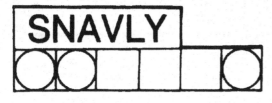
SNAVLY

WHAT HE SAID WHEN THE PSYCHIATRIST ASKED WHETHER HE HAD TROUBLE MAKING UP HIS MIND.

Now arrange the circled letters to form the surprise answer, as suggested by the above cartoon.

Print answer here

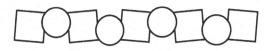

JUMBLE®

Unscramble these four Jumbles, one letter to each
square, to form four ordinary words.

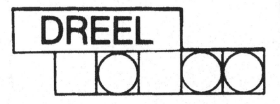
DREEL

VERPO

UNCLOM

SCOFIA

THUD!

HOW TO KEEP
FROM FALLING
OUT OF BED.

Now arrange the circled letters to form the surprise
answer, as suggested by the above cartoon.

*Print answer
here*

ON THE

JUMBLE®

Unscramble these four Jumbles, one letter to each
square, to form four ordinary words.

VOARB

MYNAL

RIDAFA

NOXEGY

WHAT KIND OF
EXPERIENCE MIGHT IT
BE WHEN YOU
GAMBLE AWAY THE
RENT MONEY?

Now arrange the circled letters to form the surprise
answer, as suggested by the above cartoon.

Print answer here A "◯◯◯◯◯◯◯" ONE

JUMBLE®

Unscramble these four Jumbles, one letter to each square, to form four ordinary words.

PHARY

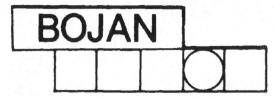

BOJAN

STAPOL

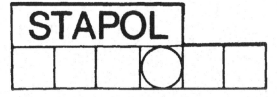

KOOCIE

THEY KEPT CALLING HIM A CRACKPOT UNTIL HE HIT THIS.

Now arrange the circled letters to form the surprise answer, as suggested by the above cartoon.

Print answer here   THE

JUMBLE®

Unscramble these four Jumbles, one letter to each square, to form four ordinary words.

VANIE

ARBSS

GEBBUD

GLEFUN

WHAT THAT NUT DECIDED TO GIVE UP AFTER READING ABOUT THE BAD EFFECTS OF ALCOHOL.

Now arrange the circled letters to form the surprise answer, as suggested by the above cartoon.

Print answer here

Unscramble these four Jumbles, one letter to each square, to form four ordinary words.

PYJUM

CUIMS

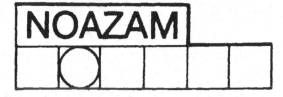

NOAZAM

MAMBEL

WHAT THE INSURANCE COMPANY PAID HIM WHEN HE BUMPED HIS HEAD.

Now arrange the circled letters to form the surprise answer, as suggested by the above cartoon.

Print answer here

A

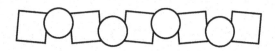

Unscramble these four Jumbles, one letter to each square, to form four ordinary words.

IDLAY

INGYL

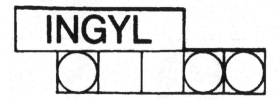
JERIGG

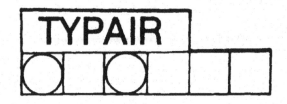
TYPAIR

YOU WOULDN'T CALL THAT PRETTY STEWARDESS THIS, WOULD YOU?

Now arrange the circled letters to form the surprise answer, as suggested by the above cartoon.

Print answer here A " ⬡⬡⬡⬡⬡ " ⬡⬡⬡⬡

Unscramble these four Jumbles, one letter to each square, to form four ordinary words.

YUMST

WARBL

YETHIG

GLIEGG

STATE LINE

WHAT THEY CALLED THOSE CIGARETTE SMUGGLERS.

Now arrange the circled letters to form the surprise answer, as suggested by the above cartoon.

Print answer here "  —  "

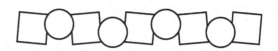

JUMBLE®

Unscramble these four Jumbles, one letter to each square, to form four ordinary words.

CHITK

HEWIG

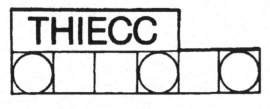

THIECC

YAWMID

Double double toil and trouble

WHAT MACBETH WONDERED WHEN HE ENCOUNTERED THE THREE WEIRD SISTERS.

Now arrange the circled letters to form the surprise answer, as suggested by the above cartoon.

Print answer here

 **WAS**

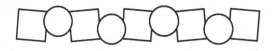

JUMBLE®

Unscramble these four Jumbles, one letter to each square, to form four ordinary words.

MERIN

MARRE

ZAHDAR

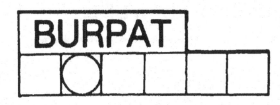

BURPAT

PEOPLE WHO SING LIKE A CANARY SELDOM EAT LIKE THIS.

Now arrange the circled letters to form the surprise answer, as suggested by the above cartoon.

Print answer here

JUMBLE

Unscramble these four Jumbles, one letter to each
square, to form four ordinary words.

GINVY

CUHDY

LEHTAH

TUFACE

WHAT THOSE FELINE
GOSSIPS WERE.

Now arrange the circled letters to form the surprise
answer, as suggested by the above cartoon.

Print answer here   " ⬡⬡⬡⬡⬡ "

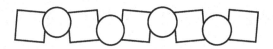

JUMBLE®

Unscramble these four Jumbles, one letter to each square, to form four ordinary words.

REXET

TASEC

YUTPED

BINBBO

WHEN IT COMES TO VACATIONS, A GIRL CAN GO TO THE MOUNTAINS AND SEE THE SCENERY, OR GO TO THE BEACH AND DO THIS.

Now arrange the circled letters to form the surprise answer, as suggested by the above cartoon.

Print answer here ◯◯ **THE** ◯◯◯◯◯◯◯

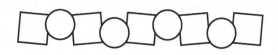

Unscramble these four Jumbles, one letter to each
square, to form four ordinary words.

EGGAU

YIRDT

RETHEN

DROINO

WHO WAS THAT
GHOST WHO
APPEARED AT
THE DOOR?

Now arrange the circled letters to form the surprise
answer, as suggested by the above cartoon.

Print answer here **A** ☐◯◯◯◯ ◯◯◯◯◯◯

JUMBLE®

Unscramble these four Jumbles, one letter to each square, to form four ordinary words.

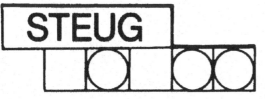

STEUG

RAAMO

GLUDEE

NERUNG

WHAT SOME BACKSEAT DRIVERS NEVER SEEM TO DO.

Now arrange the circled letters to form the surprise answer, as suggested by the above cartoon.

Print answer here

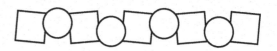

JUMBLE®

Unscramble these four Jumbles, one letter to each square, to form four ordinary words.

TUBOD

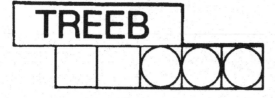
TREEB

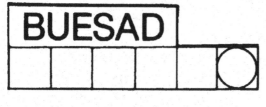
BUESAD

INGOHM

WOULD YOU EXPECT A MAN WHO HAS A FINGER IN A BIG TRANSPORTATION DEAL TO DO THIS?

Now arrange the circled letters to form the surprise answer, as suggested by the above cartoon.

Print answer here
 A

JUMBLE®

Unscramble these four Jumbles, one letter to each
square, to form four ordinary words.

DEGEH

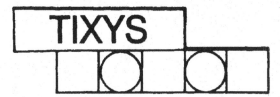

TIXYS

GIZZAG

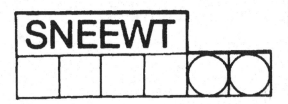

SNEEWT

We'll take it!

FOR A SWEATER, HE
THOUGHT THIS WAS
THE RIGHT SIZE.

Now arrange the circled letters to form the surprise
answer, as suggested by the above cartoon.

Print answer here **THE**

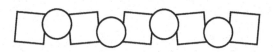

JUMBLE

Unscramble these four Jumbles, one letter to each square, to form four ordinary words.

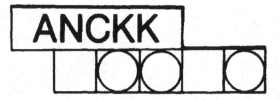

ANCKK

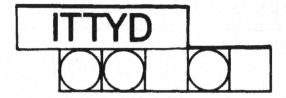

ITTYD

PROOCE

FITHES

HOW TO BRIGHTEN UP YOUR BOYFRIEND'S EVENING.

Now arrange the circled letters to form the surprise answer, as suggested by the above cartoon.

Print answer here

THE

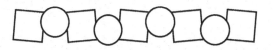

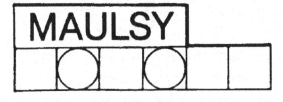

JUMBLE®

Unscramble these four Jumbles, one letter to each
square, to form four ordinary words.

HEMIC

RUYLS

MAULSY

TIBBEG

He'll be sorry

WHAT IGNORANCE
AT THE BEACH
COULD BE.

Now arrange the circled letters to form the surprise
answer, as suggested by the above cartoon.

Print answer here   " ⬭⬭⬭⬭⬭ – ⬭⬭⬭ "

Unscramble these four Jumbles, one letter to each
square, to form four ordinary words.

CADYE

FREGI

MIRVEN

PICTES

WHAT THE WHEELMAN
OF THE GETAWAY
CAR WAS.

Now arrange the circled letters to form the surprise
answer, as suggested by the above cartoon.

*Print answer
here* A " ◯◯◯◯ " ◯◯◯◯◯◯

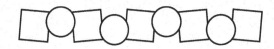

JUMBLE

Unscramble these four Jumbles, one letter to each
square, to form four ordinary words.

SOOME

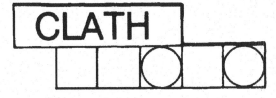

CLATH

TALFOA

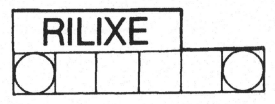

RILIXE

She sure
LOOKS young

How does she
manage it?

HOW SHE KEEPS
HER AGE.

Now arrange the circled letters to form the surprise
answer, as suggested by the above cartoon.

Print answer here

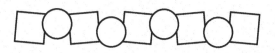

Unscramble these four Jumbles, one letter to each square, to form four ordinary words.

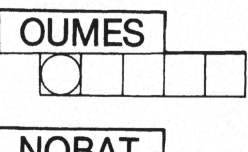

OUMES

NOBAT

LURPPE

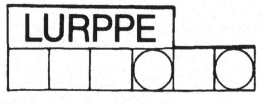

THERE'S THAT ONE FEATURE ABOUT HIS NEW CAR THAT'S GUARANTEED TO LAST A LIFETIME.

YURGAS

Now arrange the circled letters to form the surprise answer, as suggested by the above cartoon.

Print answer here **THE**

JUMBLE®

Unscramble these four Jumbles, one letter to each square, to form four ordinary words.

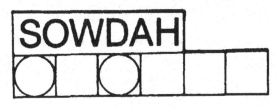

RESEA

YAHIR

VOALAW

SOWDAH

WHY SHE CRITICIZED HIM FOR STARTING OFF ON THE WRONG FOOT.

Now arrange the circled letters to form the surprise answer, as suggested by the above cartoon.

Print answer here

IT ☐☐☐ ☐☐☐☐

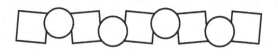

JUMBLE®

Unscramble these four Jumbles, one letter to each
square, to form four ordinary words.

NAGIT

PHRAC

CEDITE

EGWAIH

SECOND HAND DEPT. | MINUTE HAND DEPT. | HOUR HAND DEPT.

WHAT YOU MIGHT
EXPECT THE BOSS AT
THE WATCH FACTORY TO
DO WHEN THE WORKERS
KEEP GOOFING OFF.

Now arrange the circled letters to form the surprise
answer, as suggested by the above cartoon.

Print answer here

JUMBLE®

Unscramble these four Jumbles, one letter to each
square, to form four ordinary words.

TOOPH

LEROD

ISSUME

ABNOME

PSYCHIATRISTS DON'T
HAVE TO WORRY AS
LONG AS THIS
HAPPENS.

Now arrange the circled letters to form the surprise
answer, as suggested by the above cartoon.

Print answer here

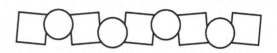

JUMBLE®

Unscramble these four Jumbles, one letter to each square, to form four ordinary words.

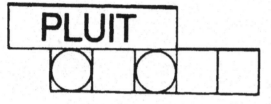
PLUIT

TUFIR

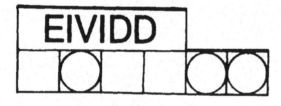
EIVIDD

BYSTUL

WHAT THEIR NEIGHBOR EXCHANGED FOR A LITTLE SUGAR.

Now arrange the circled letters to form the surprise answer, as suggested by the above cartoon.

Print answer here A

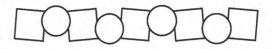

JUMBLE®

Unscramble these four Jumbles, one letter to each
square, to form four ordinary words.

ANIFT

CHAPT

RASTIE

WISDON

WHAT THEY USUALLY ASK FOR WHEN YOU HAVE EVERY INTENTION OF PAYING YOUR INCOME TAX WITH A SMILE.

Now arrange the circled letters to form the surprise
answer, as suggested by the above cartoon.

Print answer here

JUMBLE®

Unscramble these four Jumbles, one letter to each square, to form four ordinary words.

UPOHC

WAKTE

YIMTID

GANNIA

Let's go out and disco!

WHAT HAPPENED TO HIS GET—UP-AND-GO?

Now arrange the circled letters to form the surprise answer, as suggested by the above cartoon.

Print answer here IT ◯◯◯ ◯◯ & ◯◯◯◯

JUMBLE®

Unscramble these four Jumbles, one letter to each square, to form four ordinary words.

KRAAP

SESMY

SWUNIE

DAHNED

AJAX CO. INVEST-MENTS

HE SAID THAT EVERY TIME HE SAW HIS BROKER—

Now arrange the circled letters to form the surprise answer, as suggested by the above cartoon.

Print answer here

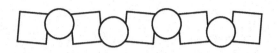

JUMBLE.

Unscramble these four Jumbles, one letter to each square, to form four ordinary words.

YUSHK

CONTH

DYSTUR

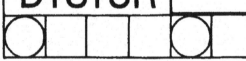

DIVERF

WHEN TRYING TO LOSE WEIGHT, THIS IS THE THING TO AVOID FIRST.

Now arrange the circled letters to form the surprise answer, as suggested by the above cartoon.

Print answer here

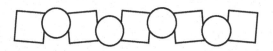

JUMBLE®

Unscramble these four Jumbles, one letter to each
square, to form four ordinary words.

KNEAT

TILAP

LAISEY

DEKORF

REAL ESTATE

BANK

VERY "EASY" MORTGAGES

WHAT YOU MUST LEARN
ABOUT FIRST IF YOU
INTEND TO INVEST
IN REALTY.

Now arrange the circled letters to form the surprise
answer, as suggested by the above cartoon.

Print answer here

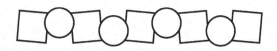

JUMBLE®

Unscramble these four Jumbles, one letter to each square, to form four ordinary words.

LAWRD

FAIRE

THALEC

CELFIK

EVERY TIME HE WALKS BY A GIRL, SHE SIGHS—

Now arrange the circled letters to form the surprise answer, as suggested by the above cartoon.

Print answer here

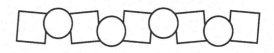

JUMBLE®

Unscramble these four Jumbles, one letter to each
square, to form four ordinary words.

YAGIL

MEERB

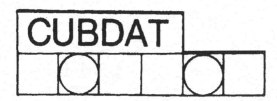

CUBDAT

DEBALE

WHAT HE DID THE
DAY HIS WIFE
GAVE BIRTH.

Now arrange the circled letters to form the surprise
answer, as suggested by the above cartoon.

Print answer here  LIKE A

JUMBLE.

Unscramble these four Jumbles, one letter to each square, to form four ordinary words.

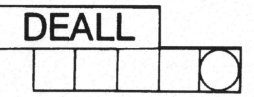

DEALL

VENAK

CAJEKT

THUSIA

WHAT A THOUGHTFUL WIFE HAS READY WHEN HER HUSBAND COMES HOME FROM A FISHING TRIP.

Now arrange the circled letters to form the surprise answer, as suggested by the above cartoon.

Print answer here

JUMBLE®

Unscramble these four Jumbles, one letter to each
square, to form four ordinary words.

SESCH

EWLEH

NAUTER

BLATOC

WHAT A POLITICIAN
WHO CLAIMS HE UNDER-
STANDS ALL THE QUES-
TIONS OF THE DAY
USUALLY DOESN'T KNOW.

Now arrange the circled letters to form the surprise
answer, as suggested by the above cartoon.

Print answer here **THE**

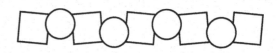

JUMBLE®

Unscramble these four Jumbles, one letter to each square, to form four ordinary words.

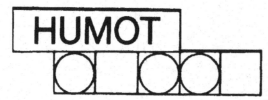

HUMOT

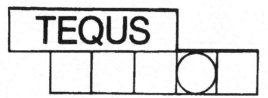

TEQUS

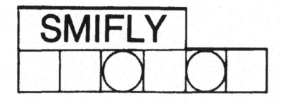

SMIFLY

BONGLE

WHAT HE SAID AS HE WAS ABOUT TO LEAVE FOR WORK.

Now arrange the circled letters to form the surprise answer, as suggested by the above cartoon.

Print answer here ◯◯◯◯ FOR THE " ◯◯◯◯ "

JUMBLE®

Unscramble these four Jumbles, one letter to each square, to form four ordinary words.

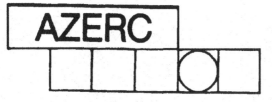

AZERC

DAPIL

TOALZE

LUFFIT

WHAT THAT PICNIC TURNED INTO WHEN IT BEGAN TO DRIZZLE.

Now arrange the circled letters to form the surprise answer, as suggested by the above cartoon.

Print answer here

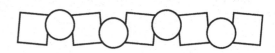

JUMBLE®

Unscramble these four Jumbles, one letter to each
square, to form four ordinary words.

WYLLO

NILAF

DARFOE

NATTEX

WHEN THIS HAPPENED,
THAT COMEDIAN
HELD HIS AUDIENCE
OPEN-MOUTHED.

Now arrange the circled letters to form the surprise
answer, as suggested by the above cartoon.

Print answer here **THEY**

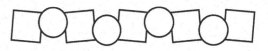

JUMBLE®

Unscramble these four Jumbles, one letter to each square, to form four ordinary words.

VETEN

WAKOE

EISORE

SWEEFT

WHEN HE WENT ON THAT 14-DAY DIET, THIS WAS ALL HE LOST.

Now arrange the circled letters to form the surprise answer, as suggested by the above cartoon.

Print answer here

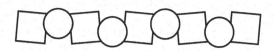

JUMBLE®

Unscramble these four Jumbles, one letter to each square, to form four ordinary words.

KEEVO

LECCY

BYDOON

DEKBEC

WHAT THAT HEATING BILL DID.

Now arrange the circled letters to form the surprise answer, as suggested by the above cartoon.

Print answer here

HIM

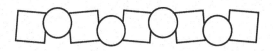

JUMBLE®

Unscramble these four Jumbles, one letter to each square, to form four ordinary words.

VACHO

SAUPE

TEMNEC

FLICEA

Let's do it again!

THEY ENJOYED THAT VACATION IN THE SOUTH PACIFIC SO MUCH THAT THEY DECIDED TO GO BACK FOR THIS.

Now arrange the circled letters to form the surprise answer, as suggested by the above cartoon.

Print answer here

"  "

JUMBLE®

Unscramble these four Jumbles, one letter to each
square, to form four ordinary words.

WEJEL

FEYHT

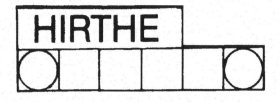

HIRTHE

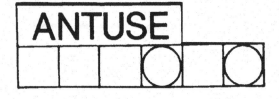

ANTUSE

IT'S GOOD MANNERS TO
TRY TO MAKE YOUR
GUESTS FEEL AT HOME,
ESPECIALLY WHEN
YOU WISH THIS.

Now arrange the circled letters to form the surprise
answer, as suggested by the above cartoon.

Print answer here

JUMBLE®

Unscramble these four Jumbles, one letter to each square, to form four ordinary words.

ROSYR

GEITH

SARATY

CLARNE

THAT GAMBLING CASINO WAS SO FANCY, YOU HAD TO WEAR A TIE TO DO THIS.

Now arrange the circled letters to form the surprise answer, as suggested by the above cartoon.

Print answer here ◯◯◯◯ **YOUR** ◯◯◯◯◯

145

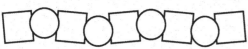

Unscramble these four Jumbles, one letter to each square, to form four ordinary words.

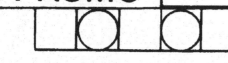
FRUMO

NOIBS

CILIAT

WHARKE

HE FIDDLES WHILE HIS LISTENERS DO THIS.

Now arrange the circled letters to form the surprise answer, as suggested by the above cartoon.

Print answer here **A**

JUMBLE®

Unscramble these four Jumbles, one letter to each square, to form four ordinary words.

FELCT

NELIR

MISOGE

SHAWCE

WHAT THE RICH TEXAN DECIDED TO SEND HIS SICK WIFE.

Now arrange the circled letters to form the surprise answer, as suggested by the above cartoon.

Print answer here **A** ☐☐☐ — ☐☐☐☐☐ ☐☐☐

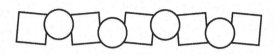

JUMBLE®

Unscramble these four Jumbles, one letter to each
square, to form four ordinary words.

FRADT

MERIG

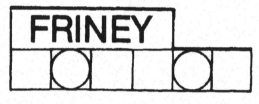

FRINEY

GIZAHN

A GUY WHO
CLAIMS HE'S ALWAYS
THIS MUST BE
ALL WET.

Now arrange the circled letters to form the surprise
answer, as suggested by the above cartoon.

Print answer here

JUMBLE®

Unscramble these four Jumbles, one letter to each square, to form four ordinary words.

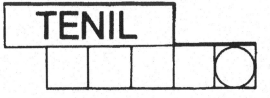

TENIL

USOED

INCLAG

NAUGIA

Look! A wonderful job offer!

WHEN HIS SHIP FINALLY CAME IN, HE WAS TOO LAZY TO DO THIS.

Now arrange the circled letters to form the surprise answer, as suggested by the above cartoon.

Print answer here

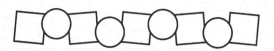

JUMBLE®

Unscramble these four Jumbles, one letter to each
square, to form four ordinary words.

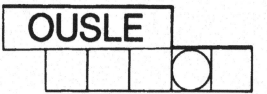

OUSLE

USHOE

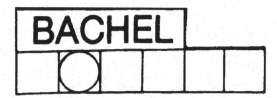

BACHEL

ROTGOT

WHAT A GUY
WHO'S NEVER AT
A LOSS FOR
WORDS OFTEN IS.

Now arrange the circled letters to form the surprise
answer, as suggested by the above cartoon.

Print answer here

JUMBLE

Unscramble these four Jumbles, one letter to each square, to form four ordinary words.

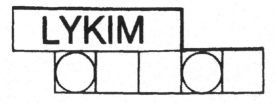

LYKIM

ZOONE

HYCTOU

GROITE

WHAT A HUSBAND
MISSES WHEN HIS
WIFE ISN'T.

Now arrange the circled letters to form the surprise
answer, as suggested by the above cartoon.

Print answer here

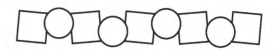

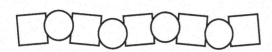

JUMBLE®

Unscramble these four Jumbles, one letter to each square, to form four ordinary words.

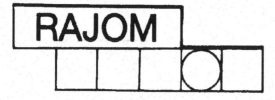

IGSEE

RAJOM

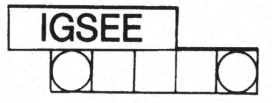

UNNACE

BALGER

WHEN A MAN BRINGS HIS WIFE FLOWERS "FOR NO REASON AT ALL," THERE'S USUALLY THIS.

Now arrange the circled letters to form the surprise answer, as suggested by the above cartoon.

Print answer here

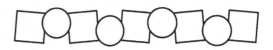

JUMBLE®

Unscramble these four Jumbles, one letter to each square, to form four ordinary words.

CUHLG

TRIGE

THRIME

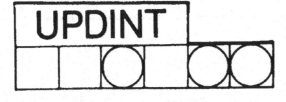

UPDINT

WHAT THAT CONGRESS-
MAN ALWAYS DID
WHEN HE FINALLY
GOT THE FLOOR.

Now arrange the circled letters to form the surprise answer, as suggested by the above cartoon.

Print answer here

THE

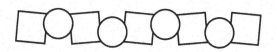

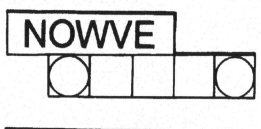

Unscramble these four Jumbles, one letter to each
square, to form four ordinary words.

NOWVE

BIATH

EEDDAC

HASFIM

HOW THE FARMER
KNEW IT WAS TIME
TO GET UP.

Now arrange the circled letters to form the surprise
answer, as suggested by the above cartoon.

Print answer here IT ⬡⬡⬡⬡⬡⬡ ON ⬡⬡⬡

Unscramble these four Jumbles, one letter to each square, to form four ordinary words.

MURYM

DRUFA

FICTEN

GLOONB

IT'S EASY TO STICK TO A DIET THESE DAYS IF YOU JUST EAT THIS.

Now arrange the circled letters to form the surprise answer, as suggested by the above cartoon.

Print answer here WHAT ☐☐☐ CAN ☐☐☐☐☐☐☐

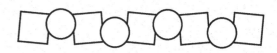

JUMBLE®

Unscramble these four Jumbles, one letter to each square, to form four ordinary words.

MANUH

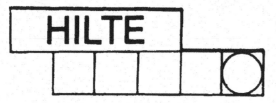

HILTE

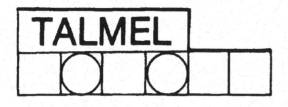

TALMEL

GINGON

They're raising the fares again

TRAINS

NO MATTER HOW CONDITIONS IMPROVE IN THAT BIG CITY, THE SUBWAY ALWAYS APPEARS TO BE THIS.

Now arrange the circled letters to form the surprise answer, as suggested by the above cartoon.

Print answer here   "  "

JUMBLE

Unscramble these four Jumbles, one letter to each
square, to form four ordinary words.

KANLY

CAXTE

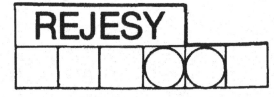

REJESY

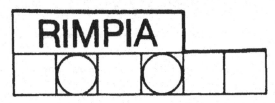

RIMPIA

WHAT THE CIRCUS
STRONG MAN
TURNED CROOK
HAD TO BE.

Now arrange the circled letters to form the surprise
answer, as suggested by the above cartoon.

Print answer here A  OF "  "

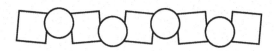
JUMBLE

Unscramble these four Jumbles, one letter to each square, to form four ordinary words.

ULIPP

ARVEG

JOLTES

THRAHE

So Jackie O . . .

Then Lady Di . . .

Here are the inside facts . . .

WHAT THOSE GOSSIP REPORTERS OFTEN GIVE YOU THE LOWDOWN ON.

Now arrange the circled letters to form the surprise answer, as suggested by the above cartoon.

Print answer here **THE** ⬡⬡⬡⬡⬡⬡ – ⬡⬡⬡

JUMBLE®

Unscramble these four Jumbles, one letter to each
square, to form four ordinary words.

LUGAH

ITUSE

HOCORB

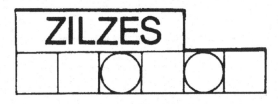
ZILZES

She told me to come here

HELP WANTED

HE JOINED THE FIRE
DEPARTMENT BECAUSE
SHE SAID THIS
TO HIM.

Now arrange the circled letters to form the surprise
answer, as suggested by the above cartoon.

Print answer here

JUMBLE®

Unscramble these four Jumbles, one letter to each square, to form four ordinary words.

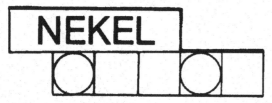

NEKEL

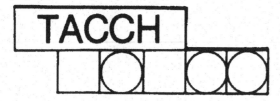

TACCH

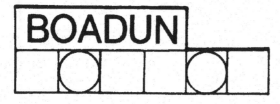

BOADUN

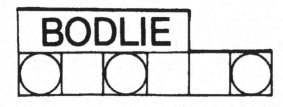

BODLIE

HOW A BARBER USUALLY LIKES TO TALK.

Now arrange the circled letters to form the surprise answer, as suggested by the above cartoon.

Print answer here

YOUR

JUMBLE

Unscramble these four Jumbles, one letter to each
square, to form four ordinary words.

TOODU

RAYAR

PRUSHE

CREBIK

WHEN YOU SAVE MONEY
FOR A RAINY DAY, SOME-
ONE ALWAYS COMES
ALONG AT THE LAST
MINUTE TO DO THIS.

Now arrange the circled letters to form the surprise
answer, as suggested by the above cartoon.

Print answer here

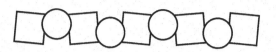

JUMBLE®

Unscramble these four Jumbles, one letter to each square, to form four ordinary words.

CILLA

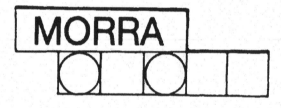

MORRA

GLIJEN

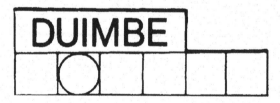

DUIMBE

WHAT THEY CALL THAT MAN FROM WHOM MANY DIFFERENT GIRLS GET LOVE LETTERS.

Now arrange the circled letters to form the surprise answer, as suggested by the above cartoon.

Print answer here **THE**

JUMBLE®
MADNESS

challenger
puzzles

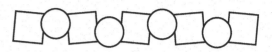

JUMBLE®

Unscramble these six Jumbles, one letter to each
square, to form six ordinary words.

TRAINO

STICMY

ENCLAG

DYLOUB

COREEN

SAUCCU

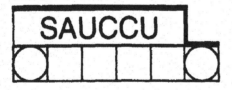

THE GUARDS
ADDED THIS TO
THE ANNUAL
SENIORS' BALL.

Now arrange the circled letters to form the surprise
answer, as suggested by the above cartoon.

Print answer here

JUMBLE®

Unscramble these six Jumbles, one letter to each
square, to form six ordinary words.

CLUSIE

RETANB

YARDOP

WEENST

SKUTEM

INBENG

Terrific!

Extraordinary!

TO THEM, THE
ARTIST'S WORK
WAS ----

Now arrange the circled letters to form the surprise
answer, as suggested by the above cartoon.

Print answer here

A ⬡⬡⬡⬡⬡⬡ OF ⬡⬡⬡⬡⬡⬡

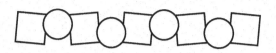

JUMBLE®

Unscramble these six Jumbles, one letter to each square, to form six ordinary words.

TENJIC

VAJILO

FRAGEO

ANZATS

DEKORF

BRILEM

WHAT THEY CALLED THE COURSE FOR APPRENTICE PLUMBERS.

Now arrange the circled letters to form the surprise answer, as suggested by the above cartoon.

Print answer here

JUMBLE

Unscramble these six Jumbles, one letter to each
square, to form six ordinary words.

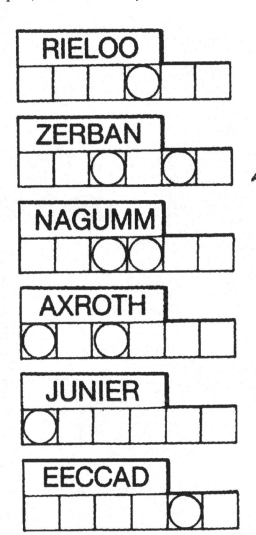

RIELOO

ZERBAN

NAGUMM

AXROTH

JUNIER

EECCAD

WHAT THE POOCH WHO
DID NOT LIKE THE
IDEA OF DOG POUNDS
DECIDED TO DO.

Now arrange the circled letters to form the surprise
answer, as suggested by the above cartoon.

Print answer here

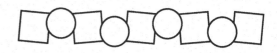

JUMBLE®

Unscramble these six Jumbles, one letter to each
square, to form six ordinary words.

BAGLEM

PLAICH

ELEVAN

CHUNAH

TICILE

RESCIB

WHAT TO INVEST
IN IF YOU DON'T
WANT TO GET
STUCK.

Now arrange the circled letters to form the surprise
answer, as suggested by the above cartoon.

Print answer here

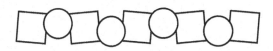

JUMBLE®

Unscramble these six Jumbles, one letter to each square, to form six ordinary words.

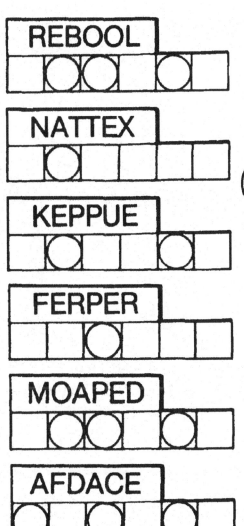

REBOOL

NATTEX

KEPPUE

FERPER

MOAPED

AFDACE

Never stops eating

Runs in her family

WHAT THE NEUROTIC COW HAD.

Now arrange the circled letters to form the surprise answer, as suggested by the above cartoon.

Print answer here

A " ◯◯◯◯◯◯ " ◯◯◯◯◯◯◯

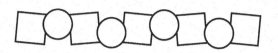

JUMBLE

Unscramble these six Jumbles, one letter to each square, to form six ordinary words.

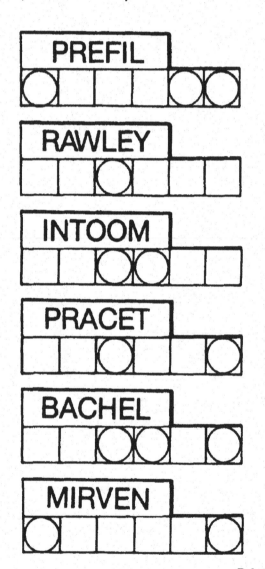

PREFIL

RAWLEY

INTOOM

PRACET

BACHEL

MIRVEN

Happy birthday, Grandpa

Who needs this?

WHAT GRANDPA SAID HE WOULD DO WHEN HE WAS GIVEN A COMB.

Now arrange the circled letters to form the surprise answer, as suggested by the above cartoon.

Print answer here

IT

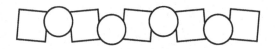

JUMBLE®

Unscramble these six Jumbles, one letter to each
square, to form six ordinary words.

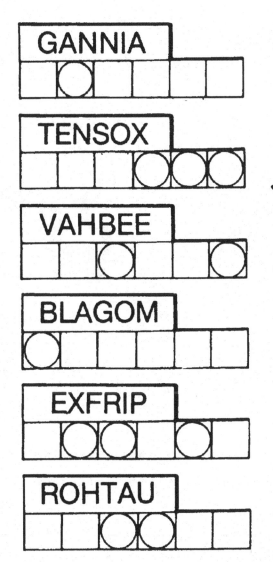

GANNIA

TENSOX

VAHBEE

BLAGOM

EXFRIP

ROHTAU

It was all luck—
no brains at all

WHEN SUCCESS GOES
TO SOMEONE'S HEAD,
IT GENERALLY
FINDS THIS.

Now arrange the circled letters to form the surprise
answer, as suggested by the above cartoon.

Print answer here

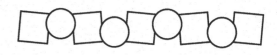

JUMBLE®

Unscramble these six Jumbles, one letter to each square, to form six ordinary words.

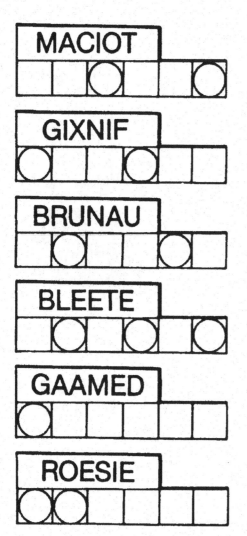

MACIOT

GIXNIF

BRUNAU

BLEETE

GAAMED

ROESIE

WHAT ARE YOU GOING TO DO WHEN YOU GROW UP TO BE A BIG LADY LIKE YOUR MOTHER?

Now arrange the circled letters to form the surprise answer, as suggested by the above cartoon.

Print answer here

" ⬡⬡⬡⬡ , ⬡⬡ ⬡⬡⬡⬡⬡⬡ "

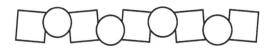
JUMBLE®

Unscramble these six Jumbles, one letter to each square, to form six ordinary words.

WAHELI

HEETES

BINNEG

LAFTOA

STRYVE

ROMMAT

A "*NEW SORT OF MOVE*" BROUGHT FORTH THIS.

Now arrange the circled letters to form the surprise answer, as suggested by the above cartoon.

Print answer here

" ☐☐☐☐☐ FOR ☐☐☐☐☐ "

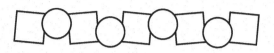

JUMBLE®

Unscramble these six Jumbles, one letter to each
square, to form six ordinary words.

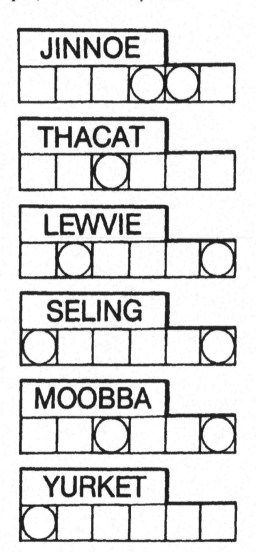

JINNOE

THACAT

LEWVIE

SELING

MOOBBA

YURKET

WALL ST.

THEY USED TO
ATTACH WATCHES TO
CHAINS BECAUSE
THEY COULDN'T
AFFORD THIS.

Now arrange the circled letters to form the surprise
answer, as suggested by the above cartoon.

Print answer here

Unscramble these six Jumbles, one letter to each square, to form six ordinary words.

BERROK

NILJEG

DRATOW

CUDLAN

BOLIFE

PONCAY

That's exactly right

Three cheers for the red, white and blue

HOW BETSY ROSS KNEW WHAT THE FOUNDING FATHERS WANTED.

Now arrange the circled letters to form the surprise answer, as suggested by the above cartoon.

Print answer here

SHE ☐☐☐☐☐ A ☐☐☐☐☐ "☐☐☐☐☐"

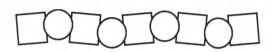
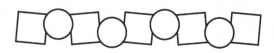

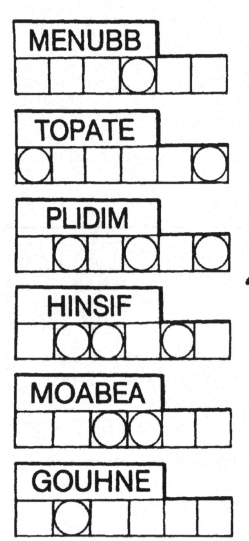

JUMBLE®

Unscramble these six Jumbles, one letter to each
square, to form six ordinary words.

MENUBB

TOPATE

PLIDIM

HINSIF

MOABEA

GOUHNE

WHAT PEOPLE WITH
INHIBITIONS SEEM
TO BE.

Now arrange the circled letters to form the surprise
answer, as suggested by the above cartoon.

Print answer here

 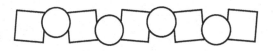

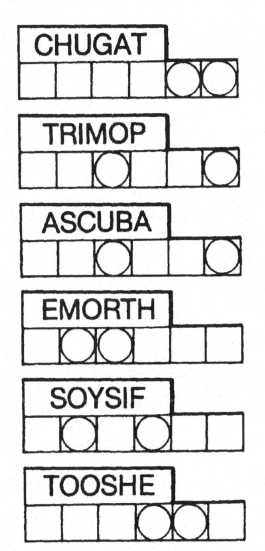

JUMBLE®

Unscramble these six Jumbles, one letter to each square, to form six ordinary words.

CHUGAT

TRIMOP

ASCUBA

EMORTH

SOYSIF

TOOSHE

WHAT THE LEOPARD SAID WHEN HE FINISHED HIS DINNER.

Now arrange the circled letters to form the surprise answer, as suggested by the above cartoon.

Print answer here

 THE

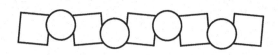
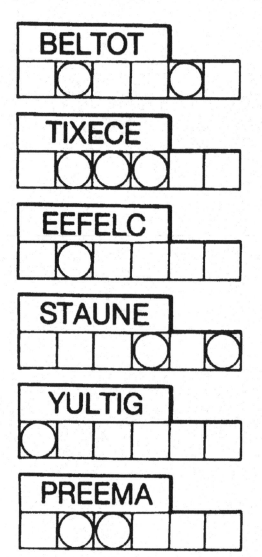

JUMBLE®

Unscramble these six Jumbles, one letter to each square, to form six ordinary words.

BELTOT

TIXECE

EEFELC

STAUNE

YULTIG

PREEMA

Don't come too near, King Midas

ANYTHING HE TOUCHED TURNED TO GOLD, WHICH IS WHY HE ENDED UP WITH THIS.

Now arrange the circled letters to form the surprise answer, as suggested by the above cartoon.

Print answer here

A " ⬭⬭⬭⬭ " ⬭⬭⬭⬭⬭⬭⬭

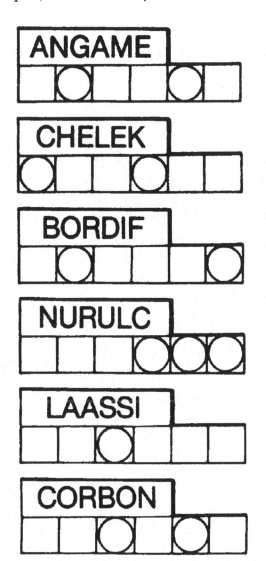

Unscramble these six Jumbles, one letter to each square, to form six ordinary words.

ANGAME

CHELEK

BORDIF

NURULC

LAASSI

CORBON

WHAT HE GOT
WHEN HE PICKED
A FOUR-LEAF CLOVER
GROWING IN THE
MIDST OF ALL
THAT POISON IVY.

Now arrange the circled letters to form the surprise answer, as suggested by the above cartoon.

Print answer here

A ⬡⬡⬡⬡ OF ⬡⬡⬡⬡⬡ ⬡⬡⬡⬡

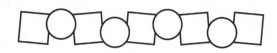

JUMBLE®

Unscramble these six Jumbles, one letter to each square, to form six ordinary words.

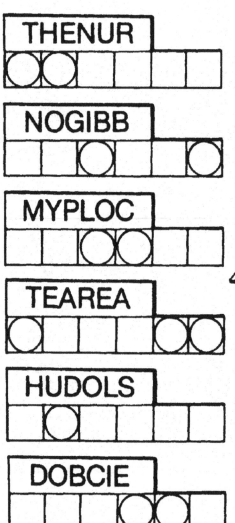

THENUR

NOGIBB

MYPLOC

TEAREA

HUDOLS

DOBCIE

You'll have to get in line

WHAT SOMEONE DID TO THE THIRSTY BOXER.

Now arrange the circled letters to form the surprise answer, as suggested by the above cartoon.

Print answer here

TO THE " "

JUMBLE®

Unscramble these six Jumbles, one letter to each square, to form six ordinary words.

MALFEE

GATHIL

TYSSEM

ENBOAM

NORMED

INGALD

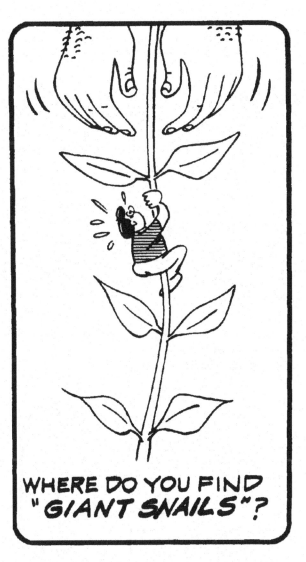

WHERE DO YOU FIND "GIANT SNAILS"?

Now arrange the circled letters to form the surprise answer, as suggested by the above cartoon.

Print answer here

AT THE END OF

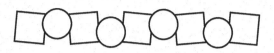

JUMBLE®

Unscramble these six Jumbles, one letter to each square, to form six ordinary words.

CASSEC

LUFFIT

DREVIT

HUBILS

PHARME

YURNEP

He's always right down the middle

WHAT THE MUSICIAN TURNED BALLPLAYER HAD.

Now arrange the circled letters to form the surprise answer, as suggested by the above cartoon.

Print answer here

THE ◯◯◯◯◯◯◯ ◯◯◯◯◯

JUMBLE®

Unscramble these six Jumbles, one letter to each
square, to form six ordinary words.

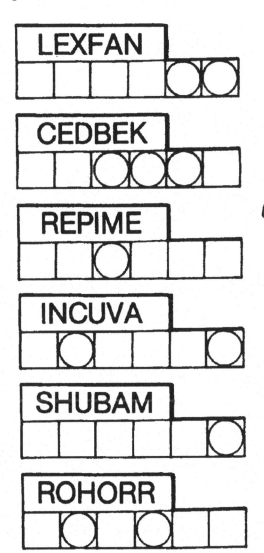

LEXFAN

CEDBEK

REPIME

INCUVA

SHUBAM

ROHORR

WHAT THAT
FASHIONABLE HAIR
STYLIST MIGHT PUT.

Now arrange the circled letters to form the surprise
answer, as suggested by the above cartoon.

Print answer here

A ◯◯◯◯◯ ◯◯ YOUR ◯◯◯◯

ANSWERS

1. **Jumbles:** FORUM CAKED PREFER BRONCO
   Answer: This blow was got from a scuffle—A "CUFF"

2. **Jumbles:** CHALK EIGHT VELVET UNTRUE
   Answer: One—that might be worth more than any of the others—THE ACE

3. **Jumbles:** GRIEF NOISY FAMOUS INJECT
   Answer: How odd that it might be square!—A RING

4. **Jumbles:** WHEEL BERET LAGOON OBTUSE
   Answer: Where some people manage to keep their weight down—BELOW THE BELT

5. **Jumbles:** CREEL SOGGY UNEASY GUIDED
   Answer: Even better than a close friend-A GENEROUS ONE

6. **Jumbles:** CHEEK KITTY BROKER LACING
   Answer: What the navy recruit got out of boot camp—A BIG KICK

7. **Jumbles:** LOUSY GUILD BEACON FORMAL
   Answer: What puppy love is sometimes the beginning of—A DOG'S LIFE

8. **Jumbles:** BATON GLAND CRAYON HALVED
   Answer: What no upright person would do—LEAN

9. **Jumbles:** SUEDE GUESS CANOPY PALLID
   Answer: Did hangmen carry out such sentences?—SUSPENDED ONES

10. **Jumbles:** PRIOR MAUVE FORGET DULCET
    Answer: Words you might get from Voltaire—"I LOVE ART"

11. **Jumbles:** OUTDO PIOUS COUPON MISUSE
    Answer: What a ladle is—A SOUP SCOOP

12. **Jumbles:** ELOPE ROBOT STYLUS FECUND
    Answer: What life was like for the unlucky gardener—NO BED OF ROSES

13. **Jumbles:** EAGLE BRAVE MODISH NAUGHT
    Answer: What you might get from a debater—"BERATED"

14. **Jumbles:** LINER MINUS CHARGE PENMAN
    Answer: Metal devices that help keep locks in place—HAIRPINS

15. **Jumbles:** PEACE MANLY LIBIDO SYMBOL
    Answer: He couldn't remember—what this word meant.—"AMNESIA"

16. **Jumbles:** LOONY ITCHY JUSTLY RADIAL
    Answer: How they bent their knees—"JOINT-LY"

17. **Jumbles:** PUTTY CANAL DEPICT THORAX
    Answer: What the manicurist's customer was getting—OUT OF HAND

18. **Jumbles:** QUOTA LEECH EMBALM JOYOUS
    Answer: What color could the blouse possibly be?—"SO BLUE"

19. **Jumbles:** YOUTH FORUM MISFIT ACCENT
    Answer: A job for someone who's well-padded—"CUSHY"

20. **Jumbles:** NOISY EJECT RANCID AROUND
    Answer: What the loafer who was born with a silver spoon in his mouth hasn't done since—STIRRED

21. **Jumbles:** AMUSE TITLE JINGLE BIGAMY
    Answer: What a girl sometimes wears at the beach—A BAITING SUIT

22. **Jumbles:** RAVEN VITAL EMERGE BICEPS
    Answer: THE GRAPEVINE

23. **Jumbles:** PRONE VALVE FOURTH CAUCUS
    Answer: How they clapped their hands when she sang—OVER THEIR EARS

24. **Jumbles:** EMBER PLAID NEGATE TANGLE
    Answer: What he had to do every time she had an accident in the kitchen—EAT IT FOR DINNER

25. **Jumbles:** MESSY HEFTY EIGHTY DAMPEN
    Answer: You might see eye to eye with someone who's this—THE SAME HEIGHT

26. **Jumbles:** COUGH JUMBO BUCKLE ANYHOW
    Answer: What that invisible man definitely was not—MUCH TO LOOK AT

27. **Jumbles:** MERCY DRONE SPEEDY MOSAIC
    Answer: That gossipy dressmaker appeared to know only this about life—THE "SEAMY" SIDE

28. **Jumbles:** AGONY FLAME DELUXE WHALER
    Answer: The witch ended up here after she did this—FLEW OFF THE HANDLE

29. **Jumbles:** CIVIL ROBIN HYMNAL DINGHY
    Answer: He had to work like a horse because his boss was always doing this—"RIDING" HIM

30. **Jumbles:** TACKY GROUP FIESTA YEOMAN
    Answer: What you might see a bouncer throw—A NOISY PARTY

31. **Jumbles:** NEEDY ADAPT CORPSE TRUISM
    Answer: That expensive country club has this—MORE DUES THAN DON'TS

32. **Jumbles:** UNITY FELON SUCKLE FOSSIL
    Answer: What some skiers jump to—"CONTUSIONS"

33. **Jumbles:** ABYSS TAFFY BANDIT HIDING
    Answer: How a boxer makes money—HAND OVER FIST

34. **Jumbles:** AZURE CHAFE AFRAID PLAGUE
    Answer: What some so-called "dinner-parties" sort of are—"LAP-HAZARD"

35. **Jumbles:** FOIST CHAOS STIGMA UNHOLY
    Answer: What the guy who brushed his teeth with gunpowder did—SHOT HIS MOUTH OFF

36. **Jumbles:** RIVET BERET ROBBER WHOLLY
    Answer: How a mason learns his trade—BY "TROWEL" AND ERROR

37. **Jumbles:** RODEO ELOPE CATTLE AGENCY
    Answer: She likes men with something tender about them, especially when it's this—LEGAL TENDER

38. **Jumbles:** GOURD LOVER BAMBOO REDUCE
    Answer: What kind of a husband did she finally marry?—ONE MADE TO "ORDER"

39. **Jumbles:** ERASE CHIDE HANGER TIDBIT
    Answer: What there was in that crowded city—A DEARTH OF EARTH

40. **Jumbles:** FLOOD OCTET EMERGE CUPFUL
    Answer: What you might get when the wool is pulled over your eyes—"FLEECED"

41. **Jumbles:** ERUPT BOUND CALLOW AFFIRM
    Answer: An enterprising person should not be backward in going there—FORWARD

42. **Jumbles:** FIORD ABATE BEWAIL INJURE
    Answer: What they called that nutty ornithologist—"BIRD BRAIN"

43. **Jumbles:** LEAKY FAIRY BANGLE GROTTO
    Answer: What spring should bring after a rough winter—"RE-LEAF"

44. **Jumbles:** FLOUT INKED NUANCE RUBBER
    Answer: Either a boxer carries out his plans to beat his opponent, or he's this—CARRIED OUT

45. **Jumbles:** FABLE CHICK OPAQUE VANITY
    Answer: Apparently, a guy who eats and drinks too much would rather be a good liver than this—HAVE ONE

46. **Jumbles:** ARMOR POISE BRAZEN JAILED
    Answer: This helps many a golfer to improve his score—AN ERASER

47. **Jumbles:** HEDGE CRUSH SPLICE PELVIS
    Answer: What he would be if he said what he thought—SPEECHLESS

48. **Jumbles:** FATAL GAUDY CALMLY BUBBLE
Answer: What the salesman said that bargain bed was—
A "LULLA-BUY"

49. **Jumbles:** GLOAT CASTE ABLAZE TEACUP
Answer: The members of the jury are supposed to "sit" until they do this—"SETTLE"

50. **Jumbles:** BLESS OUNCE TAWDRY COHORT
Answer: How a nest egg must be feathered—
WITH CASH "DOWN"

51. **Jumbles:** GROIN POUCH AWEIGH UNLESS
Answer: The only thing that kept him from making a fast buck at the race track—A SLOW HORSE

52. **Jumbles:** COLIC HOIST ENCAMP BOLERO
Answer: What pierces your ear without leaving a hole?—NOISE

53. **Jumbles:** ICING BALMY GIBLET APIECE
Answer: He told them he was just what the doctor ordered—
A BIG PILL

54. **Jumbles:** DEMON PANIC ARTFUL USEFUL
Answer: What the tow truck was trying to do at the auto race—
PULL A FAST ONE

55. **Jumbles:** FUROR TROTH BLAZER INDIGO
Answer: What an exciting "match" will do for the fans—
LIGHT A FIRE

56. **Jumbles:** FRAUD GOURD YEOMAN BUNION
Answer: The rules for making money won't work unless—
YOU DO

57. **Jumbles:** MAXIM DUSKY MIDWAY KETTLE
Answer: The embezzler's favorite morning drink—
"SKIMMED" MILK

58. **Jumbles:** TOKEN BURLY DECENT DISMAL
Answer: What the lottery-winning realtor considered his property puchase—"LOTS" OF LUCK

59. **Jumbles:** SAUTE CURVE BELFRY DEVICE
Answer: When they watched the steelworkers the crowd was—
RIVETED

60. **Jumbles:** CHALK PROVE FORGET HORROR
Answer: What the cop moonlighting as an actor was known as—
A REAL TROOPER

61. **Jumbles:** LEAFY NIECE STYLUS MUSTER
Answer: What new actors become a part of—
THE CAST SYSTEM

62. **Jumbles:** IRATE MERGE MORTAR QUENCH
Answer: What the tennis pro finally did—MET HIS "MATCH"

63. **Jumbles:** PAGAN LEGAL RENDER MEADOW
Answer: What the cowboys called their cook—
THE LONE RANGE-R

64. **Jumbles:** WHISK TAWNY LADING MORBID
Answer: Where money goes when the plumber comes—
DOWN THE DRAIN

65. **Jumbles:** LISLE PRIZE BROOCH ENTAIL
Answer: Teaching kids to save is this—"CENTSIBLE"

66. **Jumbles:** TACKY ICING DROWSY CALMLY
Answer: Often seen at a model home—WALK-INS

67. **Jumbles:** UNITY CHAMP HANDLE LIKELY
Answer: What the caring baker liked to do—
HELP THE "KNEADY"

68. **Jumbles:** AIDED TRYST CUDGEL FLIMSY
Answer: Why the child prodigy enjoyed his birthday—
HE WAS "GIFTED"

69. **Jumbles:** WINCE SWORD PATTER PESTLE
Answer: What the worker got for signing up charge card customers—LOTS OF CREDIT

70. **Jumbles:** LOUSE FORCE WEASEL SNAPPY
Answer: The reason he won the bowling match—
HE WAS ON A ROLL

71. **Jumbles:** CLOVE BLANK FESTAL IMPOSE
Answer: What the diner at the fish restaurant had lots of—
BONES TO PICK

72. **Jumbles:** SWASH GUMMY AERATE FINITE
Answer: When the fog clears up, it won't be this—"MIST"

73. **Jumbles:** NIECE TRULY GRAVEN WEDGED
Answer: What the swimming pool contractor did when business fell off—WENT UNDER

74. **Jumbles:** EATEN BURST FABLED MUSTER
Answer: "Who raided my vegetable patch?"—"BEETS" ME

75. **Jumbles:** TITLE ESSAY DECENT MEMOIR
Answer: "MEETS ESTEEM"

76. **Jumbles:** HURRY GIVEN JAGGED ALPACA
Answer: What many expenses connected with the dairy business might be—"IN CURD"

77. **Jumbles:** EAGLE MOTIF BEWARE GENDER
Answer: What the cattle raiser did when he got a bum steer—
BEEFED ABOUT IT

78. **Jumbles:** BROIL JETTY NICETY TRIBAL
Answer: Might describe the feeling you sometimes get when a plane descends—"EAR-RY"

79. **Jumbles:** NOBLE BAKED FOURTH IMPUGN
Answer: What knocking a ball through a window might be—
"PANEFUL"

80. **Jumbles:** CREEK ODIUM INJECT FORGET
Answer: What the mouse said when his tail got caught in the trap—THAT'S THE END OF ME!

81. **Jumbles:** BOWER TARDY INFLUX CODGER
Answer: What the tailor called her partner—HIS "ALTER" EGO

82. **Jumbles:** KNIFE CHALK ACCENT BUSHEL
Answer: What you'd expect people with no money in the bank to write—BLANK CHECKS

83. **Jumbles:** SUEDE MEALY JURIST KILLER
Answer: What those coin collectors always got together for—
OLD DIME'S SAKE

84. **Jumbles:** LOONY PAPER MOTHER LADING
Answer: A doctor who specializes in this often starts from scratch—DERMATOLOGY

85. **Jumbles:** TRACT CHIDE BECALM GOATEE
Answer: The fish refused to eat the worm on the hook because he was afraid there might be this—A CATCH TO IT

86. **Jumbles:** EXPEL FEVER SUBURB AGHAST
Answer: The newspaperman turned dry cleaner because he didn't believe in this—A "FREE" PRESS

87. **Jumbles:** CUBIC PYLON GARLIC DEVICE
Answer: Certainly an occasion for eating out—A PICNIC

88. **Jumbles:** HONOR BEFOG LOUNGE BUREAU
Answer: The fellow who used to race cars quit because he could no longer do this—RUN FAST ENOUGH

89. **Jumbles:** GUISE FETID BIGAMY FACTOR
Answer: What he said when he heard his neighbor had bought one of those new computers—IT FIGURES!

90. **Jumbles:** NUTTY FLORA WISDOM DEBATE
Answer: What that filibuster in the Senate was throwing—
HIS "WAIT" AROUND

91. **Jumbles:** STEED CHAOS VIRTUE SNUGLY
Answer: What did the snake write at the end of his letter?—
LOVE & HISSES

92. **Jumbles:** PLUME KAPOK IMPEDE SCHOOL
Answer: What the timid soul finally did when his bicycle wheel collapsed—"SPOKE" UP

93. **Jumbles:** AZURE CLOTH BARIUM ELICIT
Answer: What the man from Prague called his wife—
HIS "CZECH" MATE

94. **Jumbles:** CROAK FOLIO EYELID KNIGHT
Answer: What a person who thinks by the yard and does by the inch might get—KICKED BY THE FOOT

95. **Jumbles:** FATAL ABBOT DETAIN BEATEN
Answer: How that busy executive followed his work schedule—
TO A "TEE"

96. **Jumbles:** AWARD PRIZE GYRATE PONCHO
Answer: You can keep those food bills down with this—
A PAPERWEIGHT

97. **Jumbles:** LIBEL BASSO JOYOUS ATTAIN
Answer: All she knew about cooking was how to bring her husband this—TO A BOIL

98. **Jumbles:** RAINY WELSH JUNIOR TACKLE
Answer: Never knows where his next car is coming from—
A JAYWALKER

99. **Jumbles:** CROWN BUILT FIDDLE PLOVER
Answer: What she gave him when he asked if he could see her home—A PICTURE OF IT

100. **Jumbles:** TACKY FINNY ALWAYS FELLOW
Answer: Some gossips would rather listen to dirt than do this—
CLEAN IT

101. **Jumbles:** WOMEN JOINT ADAGIO OUTBID
Answer: What some husbands would like to do when their wives go to the country—"GO TO TOWN"

102. **Jumbles:** BATHE POUND ELEVEN SYLVAN
Answer: What he said when the psychiatrist asked whether he had trouble making up his mind—"YES AND NO"

103. **Jumbles:** ELDER PROVE COLUMN FIASCO
Answer: How to keep from falling out of bed—
SLEEP ON THE FLOOR

104. **Jumbles:** BRAVO MANLY AFRAID OXYGEN
Answer: What kind of experience might it be when you gamble away the rent money?—A "MOVING" ONE

105. **Jumbles:** HARPY BANJO POSTAL COOKIE
Answer: They kept calling him a crackpot until he hit this—
THE JACKPOT

106. **Jumbles:** NAIVE BRASS BEDBUG ENGULF
Answer: What that nut decided to give up after reading about the bad effects of alcohol—READING

107. **Jumbles:** JUMPY MUSIC AMAZON EMBALM
Answer: What the insurance company paid him when he bumped his head—A LUMP SUM

108. **Jumbles:** DAILY LYING JIGGER PARITY
Answer: You wouldn't call that pretty stewardess this, would you?—A "PLANE" GIRL

109. **Jumbles:** MUSTY BRAWL EIGHTY GIGGLE
Answer: What they called those cigarette smugglers–
"BUTT-LEGGERS"

110. **Jumbles:** THICK WEIGH HECTIC MIDWAY
Answer: What Macbeth wondered when he encountered the three weird sisters—WHICH WAS WITCH

111. **Jumbles:** MINER REARM HAZARD ABRUPT
Answer: People who sing like a canary seldom eat like this—
A BIRD

112. **Jumbles:** VYING DUCHY HEALTH FAUCET
Answer: What those feline gossips were—"CATTY"

113. **Jumbles:** EXERT CASTE DEPUTY BOBBIN
Answer: When it comes to vacations, a girl can go to the mountains and see the scenery, or go to the beach and do this—
BE THE SCENERY

114. **Jumbles:** GAUGE DIRTY NETHER INDOOR
Answer: Who was that ghost who appeared at the door?—
A DEAD RINGER

115. **Jumbles:** GUEST AROMA DELUGE GUNNER
Answer: What some backseat drivers never seem to do—
RUN OUT OF GAS

116. **Jumbles:** DOUBT BERET ABUSED HOMING
Answer: Would you expect a man who has a finger in a big transportation deal to do this?—THUMB A RIDE

117. **Jumbles:** HEDGE SIXTY ZIGZAG NEWEST
Answer: For a sweater, he thought this was the right size—
THE TIGHT SIZE

118. **Jumbles:** KNACK DITTY COOPER FETISH
Answer: How to brighten up your boyfriend's evening—
SIT IN THE DARK

119. **Jumbles:** CHIME SURLY ASYLUM GIBBET
Answer: What ignorance at the beach could be—"BLISS-TER"

120. **Jumbles:** DECAY GRIEF VERMIN SEPTIC
Answer: What the wheelman of the getaway car was—
A "SAFE" DRIVER

121. **Jumbles:** MOOSE LATCH AFLOAT ELIXIR
Answer: How she keeps her age—TO HERSELF

122. **Jumbles:** MOUSE BATON PURPLE SUGARY
Answer: There's that one feature about his new car that's guaranteed to last a lifetime—THE PAYMENTS

123. **Jumbles:** ERASE HAIRY AVOWAL SHADOW
Answer: Why she criticized him for starting off on the wrong foot—IT WAS <u>HERS</u>

124. **Jumbles:** GIANT PARCH DECEIT AWEIGH
Answer: What you might expect the boss at the watch factory to do when the workers keep goofing off—WATCH

125. **Jumbles:** PHOTO OLDER MISUSE BEMOAN
Answer: Psychiatrists don't have to worry as long as this happens—OTHERS DO

126. **Jumbles:** TULIP FRUIT DIVIDE SUBTLY
Answer: What their neighbor exchanged for a little sugar—
A LITTLE "DIRT"

127. **Jumbles:** FAINT PATCH SATIRE DISOWN
Answer: What they usually ask for when you have every intention of paying your income tax with a smile—CASH INSTEAD

128. **Jumbles:** POUCH TWEAK DIMITY ANGINA
Answer: What happened to his get-up-and-go?—
IT GOT UP & WENT

129. **Jumbles:** PARKA MESSY UNWISE HANDED
Answer: He said that every time he saw his broker—HE WAS

130. **Jumbles:** HUSKY NOTCH STURDY FERVID
Answer: When trying to lose weight, this is the thing to avoid first—SECONDS

131. **Jumbles:** TAKEN PLAIT EASILY FORKED
Answer: What you must learn about first if yout intend to invest in realty—REALITY

132. **Jumbles:** DRAWL AFIRE CHALET FICKLE
Answer: Every time he walks by a girl, she sighs—WITH RELIEF

133. **Jumbles:** GAILY EMBER ABDUCT BEADLE
Answer: What he did the day his wife gave birth—
CRIED LIKE A BABY

134. **Jumbles:** LADLE KNAVE JACKET HIATUS
Answer: What a thoughtful wife has ready when her husband comes home from a fishing trip—A STEAK

135. **Jumbles:** CHESS WHEEL NATURE COBALT
Answer: What a politician who claims he understands all the questions of the day usually doesn't know—THE ANSWERS

136. **Jumbles:** MOUTH QUEST FLIMSY BELONG
Answer: What he said as he was about to leave for work—
TIME FOR THE "BUSS"

137. **Jumbles:** CRAZE PLAID ZEALOT FITFUL
Answer: What that picnic turned into when it began to drizzle—
A FIZZLE

138. **Jumbles:** LOWLY FINAL FEDORA EXTANT
Answer: When this happened, that comedian held his audience open-mouthed—THEY ALL YAWNED

139. **Jumbles:** EVENT AWOKE SOIREE FEWEST
Answer: When he went on that 14-day diet, this was all he lost—
TWO WEEKS

140. **Jumbles:** EVOKE CYCLE NOBODY BEDECK
Answer: What that heating bill did—KNOCKED HIM COLD

141. **Jumbles:** HAVOC PAUSE CEMENT FACILE
Answer: They enjoyed that vacation in the South Pacific so much that they decided to go back for this—"SAMOA" (some more)

142. **Jumbles:** JEWEL HEFTY HITHER UNSEAT
Answer: It's good manners to try to make your guests feel at home, especially when you wish this—THEY WERE

143. **Jumbles:** SORRY EIGHT ASTRAY LANCER
Answer: That gambling casino was so fancy, you had to wear a tie to do this—LOSE YOUR SHIRT

144. **Jumbles:** FORUM BISON ITALIC HAWKER
Answer: He fiddles while his listeners do this—A SLOW BURN

145. **Jumbles:** CLEFT LINER EGOISM CASHEW
Answer: What the rich Texan decided to send his sick wife—A GET-WELL CAR

146. **Jumbles:** DRAFT GRIME FINERY HAZING
Answer: A guy who claims he's always this must be all wet—RIGHT AS RAIN

147. **Jumbles:** INLET DOUSE LACING IGUANA
Answer: When his ship finally came in, he was too lazy to do this—UNLOAD IT

148. **Jumbles:** LOUSE HOUSE BLEACH GROTTO
Answer: What a guy who's never at a loss for words often is—OUR LOSS

149. **Jumbles:** MILKY OZONE TOUCHY GOITER
Answer: What a husband misses when his wife isn't—HOME COOKING

150. **Jumbles:** SIEGE MAJOR NUANCE GARBLE
Answer: When a man brings his wife flowers for "no reason at all," there's usually this—A REASON

151. **Jumbles:** GULCH TIGER HERMIT PUNDIT
Answer: What that congressman always did when he finally got the floor—HIT THE CEILING

152. **Jumbles:** WOVEN HABIT DECADE FAMISH
Answer: How the farmer knew it was time to get up—IT DAWNED ON HIM

153. **Jumbles:** RUMMY FRAUD INFECT OBLONG
Answer: It's easy to stick to a diet these days if you just eat this—WHAT YOU CAN AFFORD

154. **Jumbles:** HUMAN LITHE MALLET NOGGIN
Answer: No matter how conditions improve in that big city, the subway always appears to be this—"IN A HOLE"

155. **Jumbles:** LANKY EXACT JERSEY IMPAIR
Answer: What the circus strongman turned crook had to be—A MAN OF "STEAL"

156. **Jumbles:** PUPIL GRAVE JOSTLE HEARTH
Answer: What those gossip reporters often give you the lowdown on—THE HIGHER-UPS

157. **Jumbles:** LAUGH SUITE BROOCH SIZZLE
Answer: He joined the fire department because she said this to him—GO TO BLAZES

158. **Jumbles:** KNEEL CATCH ABOUND BOILED
Answer: How a barber usually likes to talk—BEHIND YOUR BACK

159. **Jumbles:** OUTDO ARRAY PUSHER BICKER
Answer: When you save money for a raint day, someone always comes along at the last minute to do this—SOAK YOU

160. **Jumbles:** LILAC ARMOR JINGLE IMBUED
Answer: What they call that man from whom many different girls get love letters—THE MAILMAN

161. **Jumbles:** RATION MYSTIC GLANCE DOUBLY ENCORE CAUCUS
Answer: The guards added this to the annual senior's ball—"SOCIAL" SECURITY

162. **Jumbles:** SLUICE BANTER PARODY NEWEST MUSKET BENIGN
Answer: To them, the artist's work was—A STROKE OF GENIUS

163. **Jumbles:** INJECT JOVIAL FORAGE STANZA FORKED LIMBER
Answer: What they called the course for apprentice plumbers—BASIC "DRAINING"

164. **Jumbles:** ORIOLE BRAZEN MAGNUM THORAX INJURE ACCEDE
Answer: What the pooch who did not like the idea of dog pounds decided to do—GO ON A DIET

165. **Jumbles:** GAMBLE CALIPH LEAVEN HAUNCH ELICIT SCRIBE
Answer: What to invest in if you don't want to get stuck—A THIMBLE

166. **Jumbles:** BOLERO EXTANT UPKEEP PREFER POMADE FACADE
Answer: What the neurotic cow had—A "FODDER" COMPLEX

167. **Jumbles:** PILFER LAWYER MOTION CARPET BLEACH VERMIN
Answer: What the grandpa said he would do when he was given a comb—NEVER PART WITH IT

168. **Jumbles:** ANGINA SEXTON BEHAVE GAMBOL PREFIX AUTHOR
Answer: When success goes to someone's head, it generally finds this—NOTHING THERE

169. **Jumbles:** ATOMIC FIXING AUBURN BEETLE DAMAGE SOIREE
Answer: "What are you going to do when you grow up to be a big lady like your mother?"—"DIET, OF COURSE"

170. **Jumbles:** AWHILE SEETHE BENIGN AFLOAT VESTRY MARMOT
Answer: A "NEW SORT OF MOVE" brought forth this—"VOTES FOR WOMEN"

171. **Jumbles:** ENJOIN ATTACH WEEVIL SINGLE BAMBOO TURKEY
Answer: They used to attach watches to chains because they couldn't afford this—TO LOSE TIME

172. **Jumbles:** BROKER JINGLE TOWARD UNCLAD FOIBLE CANOPY
Answer: How Betsy Ross knew what the Founding Fathers wanted—SHE TOOK A FLAG "POLL"

173. **Jumbles:** BENUMB TEAPOT LIMPID FINISH AMOEBA ENOUGH
Answer: What people with inhibitions seem to be—TIED UP IN "NOTS"

174. **Jumbles:** CAUGHT IMPORT ABACUS MOTHER OSSIFY SOOTHE
Answer: What did the leopard say when he finished his dinner?—THAT HIT THE SPOTS

175. **Jumbles:** BOTTLE EXCITE FLEECE UNSEAT GUILTY AMPERE
Answer: Anything he touched turned to gold, which is why he ended up with this—A "GILT" COMPLEX

176. **Jumbles:** MANAGE HECKLE FORBID UNCURL ASSAIL BRONCO
Answer: What he got when he picked a four-leaf clover growing in the midst of all that poison ivy—A RASH OF GOOD LUCK

177. **Jumbles:** HUNTER GIBBON COMPLY AERATE SHOULD BODICE
Answer: What someone did to the thirsty boxer—BEAT HIM TO THE "PUNCH"

178. **Jumbles:** FEMALE ALIGHT SYSTEM BEMOAN MODERN LADING
Answer: Where do you find "giant snails?"—AT THE END OF GIANTS' FINGERS

179. **Jumbles:** ACCESS FITFUL DIVERT BLUISH HAMPER PENURY
Answer: : What the musician turned ballplayer had—THE PERFECT PITCH

180. **Jumbles:** FLAXEN BEDECK EMPIRE VICUNA AMBUSH HORROR
Answer: What that fashionable hair stylist might put—A PRICE ON YOUR HEAD

Need More Jumbles®?

Order any of these books through your bookseller or call Triumph Books toll-free at 800-888-4741.

Jumble® Books

More than 175 puzzles each!

Cowboy Jumble®
$10.95 • ISBN: 978-1-62937-355-3

Jammin' Jumble®
$9.95 • ISBN: 978-1-57243-844-6

Java Jumble®
$10.95 • ISBN: 978-1-60078-415-6

Jet Set Jumble®
$9.95 • ISBN: 978-1-60078-353-1

Jolly Jumble®
$10.95 • ISBN: 978-1-60078-214-5

Jumble® Anniversary
$10.95 • ISBN: 987-1-62937-734-6

Jumble® Ballet
$10.95 • ISBN: 978-1-62937-616-5

Jumble® Birthday
$10.95 • ISBN: 978-1-62937-652-3

Jumble® Celebration
$10.95 • ISBN: 978-1-60078-134-6

Jumble® Champion
$10.95 • ISBN: 978-1-62937-870-1

Jumble® Cuisine
$10.95 • ISBN: 978-1-62937-735-3

Jumble® Drag Race
$9.95 • ISBN: 978-1-62937-483-3

Jumble® Ever After
$10.95 • ISBN: 978-1-62937-785-8

Jumble® Explorer
$9.95 • ISBN: 978-1-60078-854-3

Jumble® Explosion
$10.95 • ISBN: 978-1-60078-078-3

Jumble® Fever
$9.95 • ISBN: 978-1-57243-593-3

Jumble® Galaxy
$10.95 • ISBN: 978-1-60078-583-2

Jumble® Garden
$10.95 • ISBN: 978-1-62937-653-0

Jumble® Genius
$10.95 • ISBN: 978-1-57243-896-5

Jumble® Geography
$10.95 • ISBN: 978-1-62937-615-8

Jumble® Getaway
$10.95 • ISBN: 978-1-60078-547-4

Jumble® Gold
$10.95 • ISBN: 978-1-62937-354-6

Jumble® Jackpot
$10.95 • ISBN: 978-1-57243-897-2

Jumble® Jailbreak
$9.95 • ISBN: 978-1-62937-002-6

Jumble® Jambalaya
$9.95 • ISBN: 978-1-60078-294-7

Jumble® Jitterbug
$10.95 • ISBN: 978-1-60078-584-9

Jumble® Journey
$10.95 • ISBN: 978-1-62937-549-6

Jumble® Jubilation
$10.95 • ISBN: 978-1-62937-784-1

Jumble® Jubilee
$10.95 • ISBN: 978-1-57243-231-4

Jumble® Juggernaut
$9.95 • ISBN: 978-1-60078-026-4

Jumble® Kingdom
$10.95 • ISBN: 978-1-62937-079-8

Jumble® Knockout
$9.95 • ISBN: 978-1-62937-078-1

Jumble® Madness
$10.95 • ISBN: 978-1-892049-24-7

Jumble® Magic
$9.95 • ISBN: 978-1-60078-795-9

Jumble® Mania
$10.95 • ISBN: 978-1-57243-697-8

Jumble® Marathon
$9.95 • ISBN: 978-1-60078-944-1

Jumble® Neighbor
$10.95 • ISBN: 978-1-62937-845-9

Jumble® Parachute
$10.95 • ISBN: 978-1-62937-548-9

Jumble® Safari
$9.95 • ISBN: 978-1-60078-675-4

Jumble® Sensation
$10.95 • ISBN: 978-1-60078-548-1

Jumble® Skyscraper
$10.95 • ISBN: 978-1-62937-869-5

Jumble® Symphony
$10.95 • ISBN: 978-1-62937-131-3

Jumble® Theater
$9.95 • ISBN: 978-1-62937-484-0

Jumble® University
$10.95 • ISBN: 978-1-62937-001-9

Jumble® Unleashed
$10.95 • ISBN: 978-1-62937-844-2

Jumble® Vacation
$10.95 • ISBN: 978-1-60078-796-6

Jumble® Wedding
$9.95 • ISBN: 978-1-62937-307-2

Jumble® Workout
$10.95 • ISBN: 978-1-60078-943-4

Jump, Jive and Jumble®
$9.95 • ISBN: 978-1-60078-215-2

Lunar Jumble®
$9.95 • ISBN: 978-1-60078-853-6

Monster Jumble®
$10.95 • ISBN: 978-1-62937-213-6

Mystic Jumble®
$9.95 • ISBN: 978-1-62937-130-6

Rainy Day Jumble®
$10.95 • ISBN: 978-1-60078-352-4

Royal Jumble®
$10.95 • ISBN: 978-1-60078-738-6

Sports Jumble®
$10.95 • ISBN: 978-1-57243-113-3

Summer Fun Jumble®
$10.95 • ISBN: 978-1-57243-114-0

Touchdown Jumble®
$9.95 • ISBN: 978-1-62937-212-9

Oversize Jumble® Books

More than 500 puzzles!

Colossal Jumble®
$19.95 • ISBN: 978-1-57243-490-5

Jumbo Jumble®
$19.95 • ISBN: 978-1-57243-314-4

Jumble® Crosswords™

More than 175 puzzles!

Jumble® Crosswords™
$10.95 • ISBN: 978-1-57243-347-2